AF718184

Crystal Consciousness
The Way Forward 3

ISBN: 978-178456-666-1
Perfect Bound

First published 2019 by UPFRONT PUBLISHING

Peterborough, England.

An environmentally friendly book printed and bound in England

by www.printondemand-worldwide.com

Crystal Consciousness

The Way Forward 3

Lindsay Ball and The Crystal Team

Dedication

This book is dedicated to the co-creation of Nova Earth, the new Golden Age, with love, light and gratitude.

Foreword

Crystal Consciousness - The Way Forward 3

It is with great joy that the third book in The Way Forward series is now published, and the set completed.

It sets the energetic intention for the co-creation of Nova Earth, a time of equality, fairness, justice, new technologies, community networking, health and well-being, peace and harmony, with the energies of love.

As the collective consciousness expands, the events leading to the creation of Nova Earth unfold, gain momentum, and gradually change the balance of life on earth.

Learning to live in harmony with Mother Earth, and all living beings, will result in a beautifully balanced, joyful, harmonious, and creative life for all.

Review

This gentle yet high-vibrational book offers beautiful insights, and higher wisdom, about the evolving role of crystals, and their importance on earth at this time. A great read for anyone who is fascinated or intrigued by crystals or for anyone who would like a higher overview of what's happening on our planet now.

Lindsay's work offers enthralling information; from ancient times all the way through to our amazing, unfolding future. Wonderful!

Claire Devonshire Co-founder of Chellenaire

Review

After reading 'The Way Forward Book 3' I felt emotionally moved by the messages of truth and beauty from The Crystal Team. Every page demonstrated how much we are truly and unconditionally appreciated and loved.

This book explains and describes the origins, purposes, practical uses, information and data storage within crystals and their many energetic connections within the universe.

It shows their vital role in assisting and supporting Mother Earth (and all life dependent on her) during this time of evolutional change towards a 5th dimensional existence.

There are practical steps we can take to balance the sometimes traumatic and fearful situations occurring as a consequence of this change.

Dip in, enjoy, and be uplifted by the positive and clear messages given with joy and gratitude. Know the part we can play in integrating the new energies to create a healthier happier life on Earth.
Know all is well and that we are and always will be loved and supported in our journey through life.

With thanks and blessings to Lindsay and the Crystal Team.

Chris Dawson Complementary Therapist

Introduction from The Crystal Team

Enjoy being part of the co-creation of the new Golden Age for future generations to live in harmony with All That Is and the preservation of life on earth in love, joy and peace for all.

Innate Knowingness within the Crystal

"In the days of what you call The Golden Age of Atlantis, the beauty, and clarity, and powers of crystal beings were accepted as part of daily life. It was understood that God had gifted and created these conscious beings into a form that was acceptable and usable for humanity, and also for the benefit of the animal and plant kingdoms, for all radiance of energies benefits all living beings, and Mother Earth.

And in this way the beauty of the crystals were admired and revered as gifts from God, and this made their sense of connection to God greater, and their connection to each other greater, for the understanding of all being part of the crystalline structure and nature of existence, and this increased their desire to work together in harmony. For with this understanding, any action or thought of a negative nature would affect all others in a negative way and eventually reflect back to them in a negative way as part of the oneness unity, so creating thoughts and actions of a positive nature would have the beneficial effect of assisting all people, and living beings, and ultimately themselves.

the gift of God

For why would anyone with this understanding wish to create an action that would be harmful to themselves even if not apparent at the outset? Any negative action would grow and ripple out and eventually return back to each individual, so the rippling out of positive thoughts and intentions would be the most desirable and effective way of doing things.

The awareness of this crystal consciousness, and shared crystalline beingness, was at the forefront of many aspects of life, and assisted in a sense of purpose and commonality, which united all souls together, and gave direction to their existence.

Accepting the gift of God of these amazing beings also strengthened their trust and faith in the universal energies, for a God who could benevolently gift these wonderful creations was a generous God indeed, and if in the planning of the earth, and Mother Earth agreeing to receive and hold these gifts, then this Plan was a great confirmation of the working of the universe.

And knowing that all planetary aspects are linked in this way, it created a unity with all aspects of the universe, and galaxies, and beyond, and increased the sense of being part of something gloriously bigger and immense which confirmed the sense of oneness and unity; and so using crystals as part of their conscious development, and continued growth and development, helped them to strengthen their bonds and unification on a continuous basis.

tuning into your crystal

When you tune into a crystal you are tuning into the essence of God and can receive great strength, courage, wisdom and knowledge for these are vessels of the light and love of God, and so you are tuning into all of that.

In the same way that you are now encouraged to tune in and choose your crystals by intuition, or inner guidance of your preferred choice, you are in effect tuning into the crystal which has the right wisdom and knowledge to help you in your chosen quest. So if you are choosing a crystal to assist in your spiritual development, you will choose or be drawn to the crystal which has the energies of the wisdom that you require for your development, and your conscious mind would not be able to do this.

You may read that a certain crystal or certain colour crystal may be beneficial for this project, and at one time this would have been enough information for your conscious mind to accept that a blue crystal would assist in working with your throat chakra because the throat chakra is blue, and on that level your conscious mind would say 'yes' I can buy into that because there is some logic and appearance of intelligence so that's ok I will buy a blue crystal, and you would be happy and then let your intellect choose out of a selection of blue crystals.

Now dear ones, your conscious minds are expanding and are more open to bigger ideas, less structured, less formulated ideas, and it has begun to be acceptable that our own inner wisdom can choose the right crystal, and our intellect is actually happy to accept this because we know that all crystals help in some way because they contain, hold, store, and release information, and may actually have something else within it that a specific coloured one may not.

And this is great improvement for you all and makes it very enjoyable to see which crystal you are drawn to for any particular purpose; you are also happy to accept that crystals can indicate to you which one to pick. When you are open to letting your inner knowing choose a crystal, so you are open to letting that crystal make itself known to you, how often do you hear – it just seemed shinier, brighter or twinkled at me – to indicate this is the one?

crystal consciousness

And how does the crystal know that it is the one, how does it know to shine brighter for you or seem to jump out at you – how does this happen, why does no-one else buy it on the day you are going to the shop or why do you end up buying it when you did not expect or go out to buy a crystal in the first place? What is it that helps you to know it is the right one and feel confident about it?

So, just as you are becoming more open minded, just as you are opening your inner knowing and tuning into your inner wisdom, your crystalline structure is making your conscious mind aware of what it needs in order to restore balance and health, or joy and happiness, or love and compassion. And as all is crystalline in structure and essence, so your crystalline structure and awareness are being picked up by the crystal consciousness to materialise into a crystal with the correct properties for what you need so that crystal may not have existed before you needed it because crystals can materialise and dematerialise as is necessary.

And this knowledge is also becoming acceptable to you as your awareness of the workings of the universe expands, and your willingness to be open to new ideas and concepts expands, and your unconscious mind filters through more information, and your inner wisdom becomes a more integral part of who you are so you will often say – but I knew that even though I had never consciously put it into words or thought of it in that way.

And how joyful is this to experience these moments of knowingness, to experience these revelations as if for the first time, but also know that you knew them already? How life affirming and confident does this make you feel dear ones; and how it helps you to keep that mind more alert to new thoughts, and ideas, and concepts, and accept that you do not know all there is to know, and nor do you need to, for it is always expanding, growing and changing as your reality changes too?

accessing your wisdom

And so back to the crystal consciousness of the crystal that appears to you to shine more brightly, how does this crystal know when to do this and how to do it? Well you will not be surprised to know that as these beings are living beings, as they are created in the eyes of God for his love of humanity, then magic can happen; what you need to know at this stage can be transmitted to the crystal in a form that you recognise so that you can link with it, so that your crystalline structure can receive the knowledge, information, clearance, healing, and restoration that it needs right now, and working on this crystalline level your mind, body, soul and spirit will be restored to balance and harmony, and you will receive the knowledge and wisdom to grow in the ways that are right for you at this time.

See it as a means of topping up your internal structure, restoring, rebalancing and accessing your own wisdom, for you carry all your knowledge and history within your own being, and further knowledge and wisdom, different energies, can provide your being all it needs to return to full balance and optimum well-being. And so do not hesitate to trust your inner guidance for it is linked to the powerful crystalline structure of All That Is to create a vehicle or vessel that you can access in order to receive what you desire right now, and as the crystals work you receive all that is gifted within the crystal, and when you have received all that you require at this time you will naturally cease to use this crystal, and as some of you have experienced the crystal may disappear altogether.

This sense of innate knowingness within the crystal is received from the mind of God who oversees all our experiences, and answers all our needs when we ask for them to be met.

Not all answers come through crystals, there are many other ways that are gifted to offer assistance and answers, and you are aware of some of these already, and as your expansion continues you will be open to receiving further ways of assistance on all levels, times and dimensions. Exciting times await you dear ones as your energies and awareness continue to open and expand.

the collective light

And these crystal connections support you on other levels and show that separation issues are but whispers in the clouds, there is no separation either between yourselves, or between the spirit world and earth, for when you are all crystalline in structure this is not possible. And when the beauty of the crystals is a gift of God then you cannot be separate from God either, whether you call it God, Divine Intelligence, Source, the Great Provider, however you choose to see this, you are not separate but are part of the collective light, the collective crystal consciousness that unites you all.

As earthbound souls wake up to this fact they will be less inclined to cause harm and division, and more inclined to work towards unity and harmony, for this is the natural state of all beings, and Mother Earth.

It is your birthright, and it will be, once again, peace on earth for you all as your collective light shines as one within the mind of God. All is Love, Love is All, and peace will be on earth.

Our greatest love to you all, sent through your crystalline beingness to shine with love and light.

Raising the Levels of Consciousness

Our time together, dear ones, creates a blending allowing the merging of our thoughts and energies, and this in turn allows for the creation of a oneness which opens the doors for unity of conscious, and unconscious knowledge and awareness.

Inside the cells of this energy vehicle are the codes for wisdom and knowledge to be revealed over time for all humanity, on all levels, dimensions, and with access to all aspects.

For wisdom, and knowledge accumulated over many lifetimes, and forms, becomes embedded in the energy system of all beings, again in a oneness that is available to all, which is whence the saying 'of critical mass' arises because it is all inherent and stored, and when sufficiently activated becomes available to all in a way which is natural and effective, and normal on a level of understanding which becomes unquestionable.

And it is this raising of awareness to the conscious level that will enable great changes to occur on a positive level.

The energies encoded in the crystalline 144 grid, which allowed for the higher energies to be sustained, will also allow for the structure and holding of the energies of consciousness of critical mass to be sustained – without a strong framework the energies would collapse into chaos and would not be maintained, so the activities and energies of this 144 grid are essential to form the foundation for this future work. And so now it is established, allowing in greater light, love, knowledge and wisdom, then the energies of consciousness can grow and establish towards this point of 'oneness knowingness' or oneness on a higher level of consciousness.

the beauty and light of God

And in turn this allows for changes to occur which open the cells of wisdom and knowledge from those times you call Atlantean and Lemurian to tap into the familiarity of goodness, faith, trust, honour, intention, and direction, for the greatest and highest good of all including Mother Earth, all living beings, and the outer reaches of your space time continuum that develops your awareness and energetic link to the world beyond your current awareness, and to further knowledge yet to be revealed. And so this process continues, with each person or energy manifestation playing their part, until sufficient energies are raised to create a spilling over into a higher consciousness for all, raising the level to ascension for all which is the essential work of the light worker as this time.

And the form of crystal energy that we work with brings in more light, more consciousness, more connectivity to higher levels of clarity and conscious seeking perception to enlighten all souls on their journeys. 'Crystal clear' is a phrase of no accident dear ones as this works on many levels of consciousness and awareness, bringing the love and light of God, the purity, the sanctity, the transparency, the clarity of vision to follow your true path to the beauty and light of God which is your original home, and your future destination.

See our patterns, shapes, colours, rainbows, energies, all reflecting the facets of life on all levels bringing you closer to the next level, and beyond, of your hearts connection to its true home, to the purity of the love and dominion of the God centre of all beingness across all times, levels, and dimensions for now and evermore. Amen.

Intuition from the Beginning of Time

"The energies of the crystals are created from the energy source of All That Is, and so crystals are part of the beingness from the beginning of time. The crystalline structure within your bodies are of the same design and matrix configuration, and are therefore part of the energy existing at the beginning of time, and as such you carry within you the knowledge and wisdom of God, the creator, and of all events since the beginning of time, and so when you have a feeling, or an intuition, you are drawing on an experience that occurred at any time since the beginning of time.

And these feelings and intuitions are based on a sense of knowing, but not knowing, which then makes you question their validity, but how can you doubt something that has been in your system since the beginning of time, that has seen and witnessed all the changes and developments that have occurred across all levels and dimensions?

When you feel drawn to a certain star or galaxy, a certain way of being, a certain way of knowing, you are linking to that experience in a conscious way, and bringing it forward to the current timeframe for perusal, and integration into this lifetime.

And as more of you release all that no longer serves you, as the energies raise, as the violet flame clears all past miscreations, so too it is easier to link to these awareness's and your trust of your own intuition strengthens, and your connection to Source strengthens amazingly.

So in all this your desire to return to harmonious, peaceful, truthful, honest, sincere, open existences becomes stronger, and your discomfort at the old way of living becomes stronger, and more uncomfortable.

And in strength of numbers more weight is added to the energetic scales of justice, fairness, integrity, honour and faith, and the scales tip into a positive state of being which in turn rebalances the energetic imprint of existence on earth at this time.

So individually, collectively, and unconsciously, you are all adding to the intention of peace on earth, balance and harmony as decreed for this timescale on earth in this stage of the unfolding of the Divine Plan.

And so we salute the peace groups, the environment groups, the networks, the gatherings of all peoples for all positive outcomes, and watch as all these energies, as a force for good, come together within the divine light and love of God, the originator, the creator and the oneness of All That Is; the originator of all life forms, and experiences, now and forever more Amen.

Crystal Consciousness

"This message, dear ones, concerns the clarity of crystals, and the crystal consciousness that is now becoming more prominent in your awareness.

When you look at a piece of clear quartz you see through the clarity, the purity, the innocence and transparency that exists in this being.

There may be inclusions, there may be forms and fractions radiating rainbows and light but the overall sense of beauty and clarity is predominant in this form. And so as you gaze and focus on this clarity you get a sense of the purity of the love of God, for it is s/he who provided the light for the creation of these beings; the light that is said to travel so many millions of miles from planets, galaxies and so on, to arrive at earth so much time later.

But you see, the light is all around you, it does not need to travel anywhere, the light of All That Is, is within you and around you, above and below you, and within your crystalline structure at all times, always has been, always will be.

And so as you look at the clarity of the light in the crystal, you can identify the crystal consciousness within the mind of God with your crystal consciousness, which is within you as you are part of God, and part of All That Is.

And so as you look at the crystal you are also looking at part of yourself for you are inextricably linked to All That Is within the oneness of All That Is. And this serves as a reminder for your unconscious mind, and conscious awareness, of the clarity, purity and innocence of the love which is within you all as your birthright from the beginning of time, and which can be restored to your consciousness for you to become a pure and clear vessel of light, and love, as was intended within the Divine Plan.

The experiences you have undertaken as part of your total life experience here on earth have created many opportunities to learn and grow in a spiritual sense. Having a physical body, and being on earth, are a part of your total experience which has allowed you to experience emotional and physical sensations which cannot be experienced without this physical form, and without Mother Earth agreeing to provide a place for this to happen.

And these experiences accumulate over your lifetimes and together with ancestral factors, environmental factors, and many other aspects, created the total experience of where you are today, and where the Plan of God exists at this time. And now with so many souls awakening to the love and light of God, awakening to the impact of the light, of love and compassion, of forgiveness and joy, then now is the time to release all these energetic imbalances, and to clear all aspects that prevent the purity of the love of God from shining out in all its glory from within each and every cell of your being.

It is proven that the energies are rising, that more souls are awakening as can be seen by the growing numbers of people joining groups to promote peace, well-being, awareness, and so on, within your technological devices (and remember that these have been created by the magnificence of the crystal technology) strengthening the link between all your crystalline structures within you through the medium of crystal technology – oh what a master plan is that, it cannot be an accidental plan, dear ones!

walk in the path of love and compassion

And so at this exciting time on earth, as you all, including your beautiful planet, release all the accumulated affects of all the experiences you chose to experience within your lifetimes on earth, you are now able to shine your light more clearly, be your true self and soul essence; be the amazing being that you truly are, and shine your light more clearly for all to see.

You will notice the difference dear ones, you will feel the glow of the collective light from all your beings shining like a beacon, and feel the glow of your connectivity through all that you do, say, and are, whilst still being an individual light with your own particular journey, purpose, and path in this lifetime.

So when you see the clarity of the crystal, when you enjoy the purity, innocence and beauty of its beingness, remember that your crystalline structure is also pure, clear and light, full of beauty, truth, honesty, and love.

And the more you release all that no longer serves you, the more you walk in the path of love and compassion, of truth and honesty for yourself and others, the more your light will shine, the easier your life will flow, and the more beauty you will see in life itself and all around, you. The collective crystal consciousness is growing and strengthening as your awareness continues to expand magnificently.

We thank you all, we love you all, and wish you a perfect crystal experience on this day, and all days.

With our greatest love till time again, adieu dear ones, adieu."

Crystal Intelligence Service

"Crystal consciousness" is a phrase that conjures up an image of something outside of yourself, a consciousness of the crystal, but in fact it is so much more than that.

Your consciousness in crystalline essence is indeed a crystal consciousness for you are made of crystalline structures, of crystalline essence, and so as you tune into the crystal energies in ever more increasing depth, you are linking into your crystalline essence with more clarity, and wisdom, and awareness.

For your inner beingness is created by these structures that hold the love and light of God, that hold all your history, your past, present and future potentialities, and so when you tune into a greater degree to your inner knowingness, to your crystalline storage system, if you like, you can access more clearly and more openly your own wisdom, intuition, and purpose in this lifetime.

Your physicality dear ones, is so brilliantly created as to provide in one package all you need to have and to know, and all other tools as you call them, represent means of you returning to that point of clarity within yourself, within the balance and harmony of your ideal state of neutrality and joy.

All the tools help you to clear all that is no longer necessary for you to carry within your beingness for it has served the purpose of creating that which you needed to know, and all the ancestral history that has created the world as it is today.

the new Golden Age

But now we are in a new energy, a new space, and none of this is relevant anymore, none of it is required anymore, and none of it need be bought into the new era, the new Golden Age. As the earth cleanses herself, and moves towards her ascension, so all beings on earth are clearing their energetic imbalances, and are moving towards their own moment of enlightenment.

For the new era will not tolerate these outward points of negativity, it will only allow for the purity, innocence, wisdom and openness of the new energies, for how else will the new era continue to grow and flourish if the old patterns and ways continue?

And so as the year of 2013 was an opportunity for all souls to regard their inner being, to regard their life and their wishes, then clearance for many people created difficulties and problems which may have suggested turmoil, abandonment, confusion and disillusionment, but we can assure you that all this was supported with integrity and love as part of their healing process.

And many souls are now seeing the benefit of their endeavours, and this provides encouragement for all to continue to move forwards, for you realise, and appreciate how much easier life is when you go with the flow, when you accept that you are not, nor do you have to be, in charge of everything.

For if you accept the universal flow of life, then you can allow that flow to create wonderful things in your life, in an effortless way that is quite magical.

And so to return to the crystal consciousness, this applies to all people, all living beings, Mother Earth, the galaxies and beyond, it is a medium that links you all, it is an intelligence system that links you all in a living way.

the living intelligence service

The properties and capabilities of crystals are only just awakening to your conscious minds, although you have inherently held this knowledge, some souls have tuned out of this awareness, but dear ones it is there.

So this living intelligence service, created by God as a means of updating, of linking, of providing knowledge and wisdom in a portable, computer-like package, is of great significance and benefit to you all. From the largest to the smallest piece of crystal it has immense value and benefit, and the addition of the minerals add to the ability to tune into your body's needs, and clear, and cleanse all that no longer needs to be within your energy field.

This beautifully packed intelligence service sends, stores, transmits, updates information, knowledge, wisdom around your orbit and beyond, it adds beauty to your life, it adds wonderful energies to your rooms bringing joy and balance, it links in to your crystalline structure to help rebalance and restore your systems to perfect balance, and it clears and cleanses your systems allowing you to take in and absorb more of the light and love of God so that not only you benefit, but everyone around you benefits.

holding the vision

When you plant them in your garden, when they catch the sun's rays, when they radiate the light and love of God around your garden, and your home, how wonderful is that, wrapping and enveloping your environment in beautiful harmony, joy and loving happiness?

Working with the energies of crystals brings you joy, happiness, balance, harmony, ancient knowledge, and wisdom to assist you to understand your present circumstances, to clearly identify your true path and purpose, and to bring in the energies necessary to fulfil this path and purpose, for this is what you agreed to do to assist in creating the new era, and all means are gifted to you to support and encourage you in this journey so that there may be peace on earth and goodwill to all men, all living beings and the planet.

Can you sense the immense beauty of life when all humanity, all living beings, and Mother Earth resonate in harmony, resonate in oneness, resonate in the love and light of God in perfection?

Can you sense how the universal life force can flow and work on this level of radiance to create this new way of life, this new way of being in crystal consciousness for all?

This can be a reality, dear ones, this can be yours; these gifts were created within the heart and mind of God for you all at this time, so hold this vision, and know it can be yours.

With our greatest love, till time again."

Crystal Communications around the World

In Atlantean times the crystals were the holders of the energy states, they were programmed to maintain this balance for the well-being of all, however when the energies began to be used for personal gain rather than community benefit, the balance began to diminish as elements of personal aggrandisement, greed and power took over from collective harmony and well-being. This misuse of crystal technology and power, and the growth of negative energies, created the eventual imbalance and ending of the Golden Times.

As you know the information was coded and transferred to the crystal skulls for safe keeping, and much of this information is held in safe keeping for the appropriate time for disclosure.

And energies were taken by new creations to other places to begin new civilizations and ways of being, and so the pyramids were created as energy balances and holders with crystal additions to hold and balance the energy to provide sound healing waves, store knowledge, and be a physical manifestation of all of this.

And so it is easier for people to see and believe that the pyramids hold this role and purpose because they are visible to you now, and as more information becomes available and people understand the wealth and breadth of knowledge and capability of the ancient civilizations, so they will more readily accept the evidence which is growing indisputably before their eyes.

crystal technology

The concept of crystal technology is still not within some people's conscious awareness although of course they do 'know' this information within their systems and their beingness. It is only their current conscious minds being held within the old paradigm which prevents them from connecting to this knowingness and particularly those who were involved in the misuse of crystal technology will take longer to make this reconnection due to their reluctance to face this part of their history and responsibility.

And yet on a level of awareness people will accept when told that crystal technology is integral to the technological revolution experienced on earth in recent years. Without this knowledge being made available, many of your systems, communications, equipment, medical, and transportational, would not exist, and your progress on earth would be very much slower, and more problematic.

The growth in the computer world has allowed for many thousands, if not millions, of souls around the world to link up with their spiritual counterparts around the world, to show how many souls are now moving forward, to show the strength and commitment you all have to your true path and purpose, to join together in prayer groups, and on-line communities, and pages to share information, and wisdom, and support, and encouragement, and this enables the collective light to shine and glow more brilliantly all around the world, and become more mainstream as you say; so talk of angels and unicorns, and love and peace, are far more acceptable to all souls on a daily basis.

As this collective light grows, so the crystal connections through all this communication grows too, all those crystals used in this form also link energies, and also grow in light and collective energy, as you link around the world; all crystalline grids and cellular structures of all those who unite around the world begin to vibrate in unison, and unity with each other, as you work to increase the light.

And this strengthens your working together as one, as part of the whole vibration that exists in the universe, so not only on a mental level are you linking when you sit at your computers, you are energetically and physically linking as one vibration of light and love; that spark that exists from the Godhead within you all, the spark that is your original nomad, your original being, is also part of the oneness of God or Source so as you link into the same frequency, the same energy space, the same mind set if you will, so too are you beginning to vibrate at the same level of love and light as part of the oneness.

linking on a soul level

And so you are invited to think and feel as you link on your screens, that you are not only reading shared words, thoughts, intentions and visions, you are not only linking on that mental level that says yes, I agree with this, you are also linking on a soul level, on an energetic level, on a vibrational level that brings you all closer to one level, one vibration, one beingness.

And yet you are all individual soul essences with your own journey, your personal mission, your personality, and your own beingness as part of the oneness, and the wholeness of All That Is.

Think about this image dear ones, think how many people in a day you may contact on your computer through your social media, your contacts, and think how many are shared on to others, and think that you are connecting mentally, spiritually and energetically with each of those people, you do not need to see them to know that this is true, and so the collective light, intention and purpose grows, and grows, on many levels.

When you are at your computer, or phone, sending out your information and wisdoms, also think of all those souls who may read this and send them love individually, and collectively, and see how this feels to know that you are connecting to them on many levels.

See the collective light growing, and expanding, and see it spreading across your orbit reaching those who have not yet moved on into the new energies which you are now experiencing. Be aware of the impact of all that you connect with and to, via these means, and give thanks for this opportunity to globally link with souls around the world.

sense how loved you are

And then, as mentioned previously, think of the crystals that allow all of this to occur, think of the magnificence of the creation by God, and the contract with Mother Earth to allow them to be formed within her beingness. Thank the technology that allows this to become reality so that you can increase the level of light and connections around the world at the very time when the energies change so that all this can occur. Is this not magical timing? Is this not perfection as part of the Divine Plan dearly beloved ones, do you sense how loved you are that all this happens at the perfect time?

And we will begin to see the power of crystals extending and growing, and becoming more a part of your daily lives, there is so much fun in store for you all dear ones, so much joy for you all.

And for all those who are drawn to work with crystals, who have known this inherently for centuries, your time will come to share this knowledge and wisdom for the benefit of all.

And so for now we leave you with these thoughts and will meet again soon, we hope. Adieu dear ones adieu."

The Master Plan

"Crystal technology, dear ones, is beyond your current capability to understand and appreciate, and yet as has been said before, you do 'know' in your inner being what is possible when working with these gifts. For if God, your Source, your provider, wishes for the Earth to become peaceful and harmonious does it not follow that all will be provided for that to happen?

When you have concerns about future technology and sources of power to drive the world you inhabit, is it not likely that this will have been considered beforehand?

When the Divine Plan was created, before the existence of your earth planet, and before the existence of humanity, then all was put in place to be offered at the right time, if humanity played their part in the experiential life on earth. And so all the events that took place in preparation for 2012, and for the 144 crystalline grid to be established in order to raise the energies to a new level of consciousness, does this not prove that a substantial plan was in effect laid down to unfold at the appropriate time?

And due to the many souls who have played their part and fulfilled their true path and purpose in their lifetime, the light quotient became such that another part of the plan could unfold, and then another part, and so on until, 12.12.12 when the crystalline grid confirmed its energetic presence and formed the foundation for the additional light input of 21.12.12.

The Harmonic Convergence

And since those times, the combined efforts and endeavours of many more souls have enabled the energies to continue to raise, to continue to allow in more light, and for more aspects of the plan to unfold.

The Harmonic Convergence, the Company of Heaven, the wisdom of the 12 Masters, the 7 Rays, the Angelic Accordance, and the Elemental energies, are all working at full capacity to continue to support the unfoldment of the plan in their own way, and through the light carried by those souls on earth who are fulfilling their path and purpose in a magnificent way.

And so to return to the crystalline element, the structure of all things is crystalline, with 2014 being recognised or dedicated as the Year of Crystallography – and again this was not a random coincidence or event – more information is coming to light about the power and magnificence of crystals.

Designating 2014 as the Year of Crystallography brought more energy and focus to those beings and their capabilities, it brought in more souls who are drawn to investigate their true significance, the crystalline energies attracting those souls whose path and purpose is to work with crystal technology into the future.

And so as these souls are drawn and encouraged to investigate, and work with crystal technology, so it brings back their inherent wisdom and knowledge of ancient times. As the crystalline links within DNA, and physical components, is ignited so the knowledge and wisdom can flow into their consciousness, and secure the link to the current awareness of the physical crystal beings.

magnitude and significance of the gift of crystals

This relationship between energetic crystalline levels will continue to develop and grow into the future, and many new properties and uses will become available.

As awareness and acceptance of our crystalline link becomes established, so a new level of energetic beingness will rise, for with the knowledge and acceptance of this state of being it raises the energy of the crystalline structure with all living beings, Mother Earth and beyond. Once souls accept their own physical link with other physical beings on a crystalline level, once they then accept the evidence and existence of a crystalline structure within the universe, once they accept that this crystalline structure covers all living beings on this planet, all living beings throughout the universe, all forms of existence throughout all times, levels and dimensions, they will begin to comprehend the magnitude and significance of the gift of crystals, and the connection of crystalline energies.

And this in turn will confirm the connection between all souls, between all life forms, and between all aspects of the universe and beyond.

For how can this be accidental? How can this be random and have developed of its own accord? How can this not be part of a Master Plan, conceived from the beginning of time to develop and progress over your timeframe to become the massively, immense structure that it is, to link all life across all times, levels and dimensions; to demonstrate that all is connected, and all is part of oneness?

And in this way, the understanding of mankind will develop and wake-up to this connection; and as has been said before, when you sit at your computer and link to many souls round the world, this has been made available and accessible through crystal technology.

It is the light and love of God that has created this technology, and created the physical gift for you to be able to connect with many souls around the world, to strengthen your perception of the expansion of the collective light, to link and strengthen your crystalline energies, to bond and unite all those souls around the world.

To add to the energies of the crystalline grid to shine that light more brightly, to raise the level of energy, and to assist those not yet waking up, that the light quotient is increasing to a point where all souls will awaken in the Christ consciousness moment of critical mass. And this will indeed be a wonderful time on earth, dear ones, and one that will gladden the hearts of all souls and change your world forever.

peaceful co-existence

For it is foretold that peace must descend on earth, peace will be restored on earth and all souls will live in peace and harmony. It will be thus.

And supporting this peaceful existence will be crystal technology. This will not cause harmful emissions, or damage to the earth, it will not harm the health of souls on earth, it will enable peaceful co-existence within comfortable harmonic lifestyles of joy, clarity, fairness, justice, community living where all are equal, and where each soul's gifts are of equal value whatever they may be; each group working as a whole for the highest and greatest good of all.

And so dear ones, do you see how crystals are part of the plan? The awareness of their capabilities, the prominence of the Year of Crystallography drawing in more souls and raising the crystalline energies in order to secure a peaceful future for all souls on earth. And who provided these magnificent gifts; your provider, The Divine Intelligence that laid out the original blueprint for life on earth.

For your souls know all this, in the Kingdom of Heaven this is how existence is, within the heart and mind of God this beautiful State of Grace is your birthright, your inheritance, your existence.

soul growth and understanding

And earth, and life on earth, are created for your soul growth in order to experience this through many forms of life, through many times and many different experiences, all of which your soul has agreed to experience to bring you fully back into the heart and mind of God, whole, complete and in the fullness of love, compassion, sanctity, and in the full glory of the light and love of God. And so naturally all will be provided for this state to occur at this designated time on earth for the ascension of earth, and the ascension of mankind, to the next level of existence for those who choose to experience it.

This is indeed a very special time on earth dear ones, one you have chosen to experience fully as part of your soul growth and understanding, embrace it to the full, enjoy the experience that having a physical body allows you to experience, and delight in the progression of the light quotient as the Divine Plan moves forward to fruition and completion for all living beings, Mother Earth, and beyond.

We bless you, we salute you, we feel closer and nearer to your physicality and your essence as each day passes, and we glory in the magnificence of the unfoldment on the Divine Plan, and await each new step forward with joy and delight.

It is indeed a magnificent sight for us to behold as the collective light from all souls grows and expands in fullness at this time. Thank you for your part in this and we await further communications with joy and happiness. Amen."

Lemurian Crystal Insight

We are the Lemurian energies whose land has been rediscovered, although like many things it actually only disappeared from the human's eye, and now as the energies raise has come back into your consciousness, and this principle applies to the universal friendly organisations who are watching over the planet, and who live within your planet.

As with the cities of light there are many higher vibrational aspects that are unseen to most people but as energies raise more will become accepted. At one time you did not know much about space or its workings, or about individual planets, and now new stars are being discovered due to greater advances in technology but they have always been there just not visible to the naked eye so to speak.

We chose not to use technology so much on earth as this was not our mission in this experience, and we were of a higher vibration as to leave little evidence, although again as humanity's perception and awareness grows so more will be understood about our time on earth.

Our special crystals are encoded with all this information and wisdom of our time on earth, and our current experiential life within the earth. This wisdom is gently being released and your reconnection will serve to work in this regard.

Naturally the energies link to your crystalline essence, to all other crystals, and to the crystalline grid around planet earth so all wisdoms are shared, updated and increase in frequency as the vibrational level increases.

universal friendly organisations

We wish to share more thoughts on our UFO's who are always available to offer support and wisdom; who have shared such advances in technology to allow for the plethora of new advances in renewable technology and food production, so meeting the needs of power sources, making power available to all peoples' around the world, and providing ways to feed the populace with healthy, nutritious food grown without the need for chemicals. For when the Cabal fails and the dark forces recede, many things will change, and new orders need to be in place to assume the continuation of supplies.

When the chemical companies cease to have the hold over markets they presently do, then new initiatives and proven non-chemical methods will be required to provide the amount of food necessary, and to ensure fair distribution for all.

For fairness and equality are to be a mainstay of the Nova Earth so all people have equal opportunity in life, to experience being given regular clean water, good fresh regular food, good health care, accommodation to suit their needs, and be an equal part of the global community.

This is what a fair and just world looks like, and how may society advance when people's basic needs are met, and they can use their talents and abilities to provide for themselves, their families and communities to work in harmony with planet earth; to resolve their locality issues and design solutions relevant to their needs. This is Nova Earth in operation, dear friends, and our universal friendly organisations are seeding thoughts and ideas, providing technological knowhow, and supporting the creation of many of the issues which will arise as the changes in life on earth occur as we move towards a 5th Dimensional way of life for all.

This dear friends, is the Divine Plan, a plan to provide technology to allow a life in harmony with all living beings and Mother Earth, a plan to create peace and harmony for all in accordance with Divine Will, and so it is, and so it shall be world without end Amen.

Crystal Highway Connections

Crystals, as everyone knows and accepts, begin life within the earth; they are part of the evolution of the earth and part of its total structure, they are not separate to, nor created separately, so therefore as the earth has evolved and changed, so too crystals have evolved and changed, and this is reflected in the crystal beingness.

As the crystals are removed for use by humanity they are holding a piece of geological history in their hands, a piece of immense significance which stores the energies of Mother Earth within it. Added to this are minerals which relate to its location and formation so increasing its energetic connection to the planet, and its evolution.

Humans have a crystalline nature and essence which connects to the crystal essence, which in turn connects to the energies of Mother Earth, and in addition, all is linked to the crystalline grid held within the outer reaches of the earth's orbit and so the crystal connection is immense.

It also demonstrates the connection between all souls as these connections apply to all people and all living beings, and thus links all people in this interconnection. As all is energy, then the crystal energies link and change in relation to the overall energies, and so all things and people are linked to, and are affected by, the overall energies.

technology based on crystals

This helps us to dispel any thoughts of separation between souls as we are all one; we are all linked in ways that are impossible to disconnect, we are all part of the same and therefore what affects one person affects another. And add to this that we all breathe the same air which flows around our orbit and drink the same water that exists on earth, then we are all interdependent and connected on many levels.

We use technology based on crystals in our computers, and this connects us through the crystal highway to each other, and enables the sharing and communication of ideas, and concepts. This connection is growing continuously allowing the demonstration of the growing numbers of people interested in peace, meditations, working as one, creating sustainability, reducing waste, renewable energies, and so on towards creating Nova Earth. A life in the 5th Dimension; a life of justice, fairness, equality, inclusivity, creativity, harmony, love, balance, joy and opportunity; a life where money is not the object but ensuring that all people's needs to live a healthy life in balance with nature and all living beings are met, and providing housing to suit their environment, and way of life.

And thus as all groups and individuals connected to moving towards this end connect via the crystal highway and become aware of each other, and the proposals being put forward to create this sustainable way of life for all, then the energetic intention increases and links to crystalline connections within our bodies, the earth, and crystalline grid, and then flourishes and grows exponentially for the benefit of all.

gratitude and appreciation for all crystals

Crystals and crystal consciousness are working (and have been working) on so many levels seen and unseen, understood and not understood for eons of time creating opportunities to raise the overall energetic level as part of the overall Divine Plan for humanity, and Mother Earth, and all living beings. And we owe them a tremendous debt of gratitude and appreciation for all their constant beingness, generosity, and existence, and gratitude to the Creator of all things who created, and made possible, the crystal beings as part of the overall Divine Plan for us all.

We give thanks to the beauty of crystals, to their healing properties, to their technological capacity, and all other roles and capabilities as part of the creation of Nova Earth. Thank you, thank you, thank you.

Enjoy your crystals whether you wear them as jewellery, use them to decorate your home, as part of your healing routine, in your garden, and see them as part of a larger picture of inter-connectedness, of unity consciousness, of creating connections through technology to like-minded souls, and to the connection with Mother Earth, and the inter-dependency and connectivity between all living beings, and as part of the creation to a new way of life on earth, in the creation of Nova Earth for all. And so be it.

Appreciation and Gratitude for the Gifts of Crystals

Crystals are living beings in the same way that you, animals and plants are living beings, and it has been proven that crystals can change in different circumstances, and are therefore active and reactive to different conditions.

As all is energy, then all aspects of life on earth are linked, connected and affected by other conditions upon earth and from within the universe, and so when the wind blows the trees sway, a volcano erupts and lava flows down from the eruption, movement of the tide creates waves, and low and high tides, which affect the locality, and the life within the ocean.

No one thing is independent or unaffected by changes in conditions, and no one thing is isolated, and so as crystals too are living beings they too are affected by environmental changes, and overall changes in energies.

The crystals within the earth are still changing even when formed, as Mother Earth herself is still changing in temperature, in movements in tectonic plates, in sea levels, in ice flows, in earthquakes and volcanoes, and all these continuous changes, and movements affect the crystals within her being as she is a living being too.

The method of extracting crystals can also affect them, blasting and heavy mining can disrupt their structure and energy balance, transportation, methods and means of making them into saleable pieces, the energy of their storage location, and finally by their destination and purchaser. So we draw this to your attention so that you consciously acknowledge the journey of the crystal to the point where you become its guardian so that in working with the energies of the crystal you rebalance its energies, give appreciation and gratitude for its gifts, and clear and cleanse it before beginning to work with it for your own purpose.

crystals are joyous beings

And this applies to crystals placed in jewellery, those adorning your home, placed in grids or used in meditation or any other purposes. This will not only create a greater bonding between you and the crystal, but will also raise the energy of the crystal itself which in turn raises the energies of all crystals as all are connected energetically. This will also link to the crystals within the earth.

Crystals are joyous beings; they are delighted to be of service at this time on earth, and can be used in so many ways to raise the overall energies as part of the Divine Plan, moving toward a 5th Dimensional way of life.

In Atlantis, they were used in agriculture, water cleansing processes, food production and storage, healing, education, relationships, ceremonies, earth healing, as a source of energy, and a myriad technological uses.

Many of these applications are beginning to come to the forefront again as Atlantean wisdoms are bought forth once again to be used in Nova Earth, to be used to create a life of peace, harmony, justice, fairness, equality, inclusivity, joy, health, and service to the planet, and more will continue to be revealed, and more to be accepted from these magnificent beautiful powerful gifts from God, and we express our gratitude to Mother Earth, Source, and all those interested in crystallography to bring this about at this time. Amen

Enjoy your crystals, respect them and their capabilities, and see them as part of the overall plan for creating Nova Earth as part of the Divine Blueprint for all Amen.

The Mystery and Magnificence of Crystals

Dear beloveds in this insightful message we look at the impact that crystals have within the earth, and how this impacts around the earth, and to those crystals in use in many ways on the outer surface of the earth. For all is planned, all is prepared in such a way that as the Divine Plan unfolds, all is in place for the next step, for how can it be otherwise? So in the greater scheme of things all that is occurring in your world has been prepared for with provision for the next step to roll out.

And with this we do not necessarily mean each event on earth, as some of the present chaos is in reaction to the changes occurring in your orbit, and not all reactions were planned but are part of the overall clearance of the negative energy forces who have kept the planet, and her people under a false rule for a long time.

But whilst each individual reaction shows things cannot remain the same for long, things, energies, events keep unfolding to bring out the negative energies into the light for exposure and releasing so that the light gains in strength, and brightness, and attracts more souls who are ready to wake up, ready to move forwards in unity consciousness in oneness with All That Is, creating Nova Earth in love, light, joy and harmony.

crystals hold the love and light of God

So see beloveds how all is planned for at each stage the next part of the plan may reveal itself and become reality, and crystals have their part to play in this unfolding.

Crystals hold the love and light of God, and therefore his plan is embedded in the crystals as part of their beingness, they are living beings with a consciousness of their own and an ability to act at the appropriate time as part of this plan.

Many souls use crystals actively to create grids, and to activate energies as part of this plan. And so the crystals within the earth have embedded in them this plan ready to release at the appropriate time for humanity, all living beings, and Mother Earth, and for the 144 crystalline grid linking to the universal energies.

For as Mother Earth formed, and the crystals formed, their consciousness and role within the plan were established to be activated at the appropriate time, and this has been done of their own action or activated by a human crystal being directed by their higher self to work with specific crystals at specific locations at specific times, and so the mystery and magnificence of crystals unfolds in all its glory for the highest and greatest good of all.

wisdoms shared with all humanity

Different types of crystals also have special roles as for example the Lemurian crystals, who whilst not always being the clearest and shiniest, hold powerful knowledge and wisdom held since the Lemurian times, and again the information from these special crystals is being gradually released and shared in accordance with the unfolding of the plan, and this will be magnificent, and help you all to reconnect to the beautiful, peaceful, harmonious energies of that creative, wondrous time on earth.

And again the releasing and integrating of this knowledge will help the move towards creating Nova Earth as the wisdom is shared among all humanity.

Time keeper crystals, crystal skulls, Atlantean crystals are all part of the unfoldment of this Divine Plan, all bringing forth wisdom, knowledge and energies of such love to share with humanity to raise the overall level of love, compassion, understanding, acceptance, tolerance, forgiveness, humility, gratitude, and faith, to support the changes necessary in humanity to move into a 5th Dimensional way of life on earth, as set in the crystals and embedded in their consciousness world without end. Amen.

Crystal Technology and Global Rebalancing

Dear beloveds, crystal light and crystal technology will play a large part in the future of your lives as Nova Earth is established, and manifest, on earth.

The crystal beings already share much of their wisdom and knowledge with those who are able to connect with them, and more and more people are opening to this ability and acknowledging the role of crystals within the Divine Plan.

For as has been said before, all is planned, and all is prepared for the unfolding of the Divine Plan, and as humanity raises her energies so this brings alignment with the crystal energies and more may be revealed. Revealing information before humanity is ready would not be in the best interests of all concerned, and so gradually more information is shared at the appropriate time.

Information from times past, and especially the times connected to the pyramids, is constantly being revealed, and the use of crystals in connection with these structures will be of great fascination and interest to all souls. Until humanity is ready to accept this information, and until there is a desire among humanity to change, then it is harder and more problematic to incorporate this technology into your daily lives. Many souls have accessed this information previously and written about it, but as humanity has not seen the need to change, or has accepted this information, then it has been ignored, discredited and sidelined.

creation of Nova Earth

However as energies are changing, and especially as the catastrophic weather conditions of 2017 demonstrated, Mother Earth has decided to clear and cleanse her own energies causing events on the surface of her being to demand that notice is taken of the issues around pollution, and global imbalances.

These disasters created the opportunity for the new technologies to be installed and recognised to replace the old fossil fuels, and highlight the need to clear the oceans of pollution, and rebalance life on Earth. As the changing energies weaken the power of those in control whose interests are not for the highest and greatest good of all, this allows for the many, many millions of souls on earth to create, and manifest, new ways as part of the creation of Nova Earth for the highest and greatest good of all.

And crystal technology played its part in your history by allowing the creation of the world-wide-web through the crystal highway of quartz used in your computers. This allowed the set up and sharing of free information among souls around the world, the setting up of groups of like-minded people on environmental issues, on sustainable technology, meditations, healing, mindfulness, community, oneness, and many other ways of uniting people globally, holding the light, raising the energies and assisting in raising awareness towards unity consciousness.

And this crystal technology will continue to raise, and hold, the new vibrations on earth, and radiate light, love, wisdom and knowledge throughout your orbit for the highest and greatest good of all.

There is so much more to come, beloveds, so much more to support the manifestation of life on earth in peaceful, harmonious ways that are a joy to behold, and we await these advances with joy, excitement, and love, and see all life radiating with crystal light and wisdom, world without end Amen.

Intention is All

Intention, dear ones, is all, for without intention the human soul is directionless, drifting and unfulfilled, and open to energies not always for the highest and greatest good.

Intention is what directs light workers to raise their energies to a higher level to seek the means to achieve this, and put into practice the learning's gained.

Intention helps guide those who work in conservation, sustainability, renewable energy, cleansing the waters of pollution and plastics, creating innovations to support community projects and recycling, supporting those vulnerable individuals or groups, enabling and facilitating new innovations and concepts towards peace for individuals and, thereby peace for all.

It is the intention to leave the world in a better place for the next generation; the intention to create a fairer world for all, the intention to support justice for all, and equal rights for all, the intention to live peacefully and work towards peace for all, the intention to reduce pollution and create a healthier environment, the intention to reduce dependency on fossil fuels through renewable energy, and so on, and so on.

manifesting Nova Earth

And for light workers it is the intention to fulfil the role they inherently know they came here for, to earth at this special time, which sustains and encourages them to keep moving forwards in raising and holding the energies towards creating and manifesting Nova Earth.

And this intention is inbred in souls before they arrive on earth, it is predestined, agreed and stored within the cells of the body and soul, and thus as the individual grows and links into their inner knowing so this intention becomes apparent, and a part of the individuals life story.

All souls have the opportunity to connect with their soul's purpose, and connect with this intention, and many souls do play out in this lifetime what that intention was, and so each person's life plan/role is different, and can be celebrated as such.

No two life plans will be the same, there may be many similarities but no two can be identical as each soul carries forward different personal lessons and experiences in each life time.

opportunities for an adventurous life

It is the desire to reach fulfilment of the soul which supports the opportunities for growth and synchronicities which occur throughout lifetimes to facilitate this desire.

With free will not all people will move towards connecting with their intention or may be distracted by life events on their journey, and all this is perfect for them, and where they are at any point.

For those who do connect to their intention it provides opportunities for an adventurous life, with opportunities of self expression, creativity, connections to others through similar intentions, and fulfilment on a soul level of this time on earth. This is not to say it is without difficulty at times but this is all part of the challenge, part of the adventure of life and growth, and you are never alone in these challenges, we are always here to bring love, comfort, compassion, and support, beloveds.

inherent knowingness contained within crystals

And so within your being you receive support through Mother Earth, through the crystalline grid, and through the crystalline essence of your being. As Mother Earth is also on her journey, as the energies change, as the plan unfolds, so the energies contained within your crystalline essence change and link with those of Mother Earth and the grid, and so you are linking to the inherent knowingness contained within the crystals within the earth, and those on the outer planes, for crystals also hold the Blueprint for earth; they contain the Divine Plan, and they contain knowledge, and wisdoms for the creation of Nova Earth.

And so your physical being is working with you to support your intention, and as you clear more of that which no longer serves you, your connection to the crystalline energies strengthens, and your intention becomes clearer, and more clearly defined.

Thus you are receiving help from many directions to support you in your intention to manifest Nova Earth through whatever direction your intention takes you.

And even for some souls, the intention was to create distractions and actions which may not seem to be in the highest and greatest good of all. Some of these actions have resulted in positive outcomes which have stimulated individuals, and groups, to work together in unity and harmony for the highest and greatest good of all, and provide foundations for more light and love to be anchored in the world, and more awareness of the possibility of living in peace and harmony, in equality, inclusivity, justice, and ultimately peace for all.

Personal intentions can be strengthened by working with individual crystals as they are here to help and support the transition times on earth, and linking with their energies will help with clarity, and intuition of intention.

We thank you all for your intentions whether they are to bring in and hold the light, to create new technologies, to create a fairer more equal world, support those in need in times of emergency, to balance nature and support all living beings, to support Mother Earth on effective natural healing methods, to support community projects, to suggest new economic models, to reduce pollution, to promote creative thinking and education, to introduce peaceful means of communication, inner peace and world peace, to suggest new projects for community living in balance with Mother Earth.

In these and many other ways we thank you for your intentions, and actions, towards creating Nova Earth and peace now and forever more. Amen.

Lemurian Crystal communication – Reaching the Tipping Point

We bring you tidings of great joy beloveds as the energies raise in line with the Blueprint for earth at this time, and when a point is reached then this opens the gateway for great change.

It is a bit like deciding to make a hot drink, you need to assemble the necessary items, fill the kettle with water, and once a certain temperature is reached the kettle boils and there is no going back, the water boils until you make the drink and then a different form is created with the ingredients.

And so as has been occurring on your planet many things have been coming together through a multitude of sources until the energies are being raised to nearly boiling point; all along this journey the ingredients have been assembled; light workers, earth angels, conservationists, human rights workers etc, etc, have been working behind the scenes making progress creating awareness, raising consciousness until we reach the tipping point of no return. Added to this the supporters from beyond the veil have been creating the opportunities for progress, sending messages of support, love, encouragement and gently opening the next level of awareness for all those who wish to follow.

Atlantean and Lemurian connections

And pre-programmed crystals have gently been releasing their wisdom and knowledge in accordance with the Divine Plan at the appropriate time to support and give guidance to this preparation. So many factors are included in this preparation, and so many of you on earth are awakening to your Atlantean and Lemurian connections which again are strengthened through connection to the crystal energies whether you consciously link to them or not, for your crystalline essence is linked, and you react to changes in crystal consciousness.

Working with Lemurian crystals helps to strengthen this link, and to recall many of the ancient wisdoms, and knowledge, and experiences of that time, of how crystals were used in daily life, in ceremonies and reverential prayer for Mother Earth as the Lemurians were less concerned with technological advances and more concerned with living life very gently on Mother Earth, and leaving less imprint on her being than the Atlanteans.

maintaining a balance

All these energies and wisdoms are becoming relevant as another ingredient to the raising of consciousness at this special time, and we thank you all for your endeavours through whatever avenue you are drawn to support this move to a 5th Dimensional way of life on earth, to bring all aspects to this point of mass consciousness (or tipping point of no return) so that all aspects of life are enjoyed in peace, harmony, fairness, respect for Mother Earth and all living beings, and new technologies can be incorporated to maintain a healthy balance between the needs of your planet home, all living beings, humanity, and the outer universe.

For planet earth is not alone in providing life for other forms and what happens on your planet affects others, and so a balance on Mother Earth is essential to maintain a balance for all universal forms of life to exist and fulfil their own destiny as part of the Divine Plan.

So we thank all those committed to this desire to create a world of harmony, joy, fulfilment, and peace, and so it shall be world without end. Amen.

Lemurian Ceremony to Honour Mother Earth

In Lemurian times, there was a deep respect and love for Mother Earth, and they regularly held ceremonies to honour her and express their gratitude for all that she provided for them. The following is one such ceremony undertaken at regular intervals with reverence and love.

....

With crystals placed in the Star of David position and a person standing at each outer point of that star, each person in turn repeats a different mantra and at the end, a collective mantra is repeated firstly by those people, and then collectively by all those present.

This can be done at the beginning of each Equinox, sunrise, sunset, and any other special time in the earth's cycle for these energies of linking to Mother Earth are all connected to the rhythms, cycles and passages of progress and process connecting earth, the solar system, universal energies, and beyond.

The crystals are prepared initially by being steeped in crystal clear water for 24 hours to gain maximum energetic input from the moon, stars, sun, daylight, nightlight, earth movements and cycles within all living beings and the earth.

During this time meditations are performed to link into the stones, to build their connection, to cleanse and prepare them for the ceremony, and to link the energies of those who will be performing the ceremony.

Others will also tune into the stones sending love and gratitude, and the crystals will be revered for the wisdom and knowledge they hold, and the ceremony they will be used in. All will be at its maximum for the ceremony.

Wearing white and carrying a cross to represent the blending of day and night, earth and the universe, people and spirit, the crystals will be removed from the water, and the area of land to be used will be consecrated by meditation and prepared for the ceremony, then the stones laid out in accordance with the design.

As people gather in reverence to the ceremony, the energies of love and gratitude abound for all that Mother Earth provides for us; for shelter, beauty, food, and a place to experience this life on earth at this time. Appreciation and respect are felt and shared energetically setting the energetic intention for this event.

Each person chosen to repeat one aspect walks to their allotted position, and after this is completed others respectfully surround the group in a circle.

A Prayer for everyone begins this ceremony...

Oh Mother Earth, our home, our shelter and provider.
We respectfully honour and give thanks for all that you are, and all that you share with us
in the name of Source, God, our Provider, we honour and thank you
and through this Ceremony we link to your energies, to the universal energies
and connect on all levels of unity consciousness for the highest and greatest good of all.

Person 1 then shares;

Mother Earth, we come today to join in honouring you and all that you are, for your process in this lifetime, for your journey as part of the oneness of All That Is, and we thank you and love you in wholeness and oneness from here to eternity. Amen.

Person 2

We love and honour you Mother Earth for the beauty of all life on your being; for the trees, the hills and mountains, the valleys and grass, the colours, the landscapes, the flowers and all that lives and breathes upon this beautiful land.

We honour all that is in the inner workings and make up of your being, and the movement of land masses, the caves, the crystals, and all aspects of your beingness.

We honour and respect all aspects on earth, thank you Amen.

Person 3

We honour and thank you for the food you provide for us, for the fruits from trees, for the fertile soil which allows all things to grow, for the food which feeds our animals and all living beings.

For the nourishment you provide physically and spiritually we honour and thank you.

We honour this as part of enabling us to experience life on this planet, at this time, within the universe as part of the Divine Plan for life. Thank you, Amen.

Person 4

We honour and thank you for the waters of life which support the existence of life on this planet at this time. For the nourishment of water for all living beings, for crops and food, for transport for the very beauty of water itself.

We honour you for the nourishment and life enabling properties of water, and the beauty, and spiritual upliftment which water provides. We thank you, Amen.

Person 5

We honour and thank you for the position of this planet and its creation within the universe, and solar system bringing both light and dark, day and night, and influences from other planets into our existence.

To be part of this creation and play our part in the overall oneness of all creation, we honour and thank you with all our hearts, Amen.

Person 6

We thank you for providing the crystals within your being, for allowing their creation, for their storing and releasing of information at the appropriate time for the highest and greatest good of all. For their beauty, wisdom, clarity and health giving properties, we thank you, and are grateful to use these crystals, with their permission, to link to your energies today, as above so below, as within so without, to consecrate this land and connect to you on a deeper level, to connect to all crystals, and those on the outer planes, so strengthening our connection to you, to Source, and to all living beings world without end, Amen.

Person 7

This is for the special reason for the ceremony so for example it could be Equinox, harvest, sewing crops or other.

Person 8

We thank you for life on earth, and the shelter which you provide for us to live in warmth, and comfort upon your being.

We honour and contract to leave as little impact and imprint on your being as possible in reverence to your benevolence in agreeing to allow life on earth.

We honour you in all ways, love and respect you in all ways, and will work together for the highest and greatest good of all.

....

At this point a general silence for a few minutes ensues to allow for the integration of energies, and all persons may silently send their love and gratitude to Mother Earth, and all living beings in oneness and unity consciousness.

Thereby follows the final prayer said by those above....

In our totality and oneness we thank the crystals for enabling this ceremony of love, gratitude, appreciation, honour and respect, for the generosity of Mother Earth in allowing life on earth, for creating the magnificence and beauty which we enjoy, and to providing all that we need in order to fulfil our life on earth at this time, and complete our soul contracts as part of the overall unity consciousness of All That Is. And we thank our Source, Provider, Maker of all things for this part of the Divine Plan, this Blueprint for earth, forever and ever Amen.

....

Then follows a general feeling of exultation, happiness, joy, gratitude, and love as the ceremony closes and people congregate for general enjoyment; music, song, and story-telling may follow.

The crystals remain in place for a further 24 hours, and can be revisited before being thanked, removed, and placed in clear water to recharge them, and placed in sunlight and rested; they will continue to release energies of love and wisdom appropriate at that time until used again.

Crystal Beings share Information about the Universe

Crystals are gifts from God to help all humanity in a myriad ways. They are preformed, predetermined, and predestined, if you like, as part of the Divine Plan, the Blueprint for life on earth.

Crystals hold this Divine Plan within their cells, and are able to release these wisdoms and energies at the appropriate time with the appropriate person, which also is why a crystal will choose the person who is ready to receive these energies.

For it is known, and accepted, that once a person starts working with crystals, and forms a link with their crystalline essence, they are ‘in tune’ or alignment with the energies.

Thus once this link is established souls will be drawn to a crystal which may be different from the one they originally set out to buy, or indeed were not planning on buying one at all on that day.

So the crystal energy will link with that energetic connection within the body, and messages are communicated to buy that crystal, as the crystal knows that that soul will be the guardian of that wisdom until the time is right for the energies to be released, and the insights shared.

And this is also the way that crystal skulls work for the essence, or personality of the skull, is already present in an energetic form although not actually in the crystal form.

bringing distant information

The wisdom and personality form links to the crystal being, and that crystal being senses the right soul to link to, and this may be by seeing a crystal on the internet, in a shop or even being gifted one as a present. A person may just feel that a crystal needs to be passed on to the next guardian – for we never own crystals, they will stay for as long as necessary but can disappear if it is no longer appropriate to be with that person or in that environment.

And so as the soul is drawn to buy or receive the crystal skull, then the personality enters and blends with the crystal being to bring forth the wisdom and energetic connection necessary at that time.

And these connections can be from other planets, other beings in different universes or other forms which bring distant information into the earthly orbit through the connection with the crystal being and chosen guardian.

The formation of the crystal into a crystal skull brings forth the concept of a personality, of a brain, vision, sight and hearing, and a connection to a familiar human form. This allows the brain to more fully accept the building of a deeper relationship which allows sharing of subtle energies and universal information whilst enjoying a more personal connection.

Skulls do share their personalities through the information they bring, and their purpose for their beingness. Their energies will feel different according to their origin and purpose.

Working for the highest and greatest good of all

And that is another difference with crystal beings over crystals that their personality of the being will encourage the naming of the skull i.e. the name will be communicated to the guardian and will often but not always give a clue as to its purpose.

And so once again we can see how the universal energies, Divine Plan and intention are created to bring forth for humanity means of healing, of understanding about the universe, about receiving wisdom, and information, appropriate at the time, and a connection to all crystalline energies within Mother Earth, and the crystalline grid, and as part of the oneness of All That Is.

We thank Mother Earth for providing the experience of growth of the crystals within her being, and to all those who work with crystals for the highest and greatest good of all. Amen beloveds Amen.

Crystals bring Love and Peace to your Home

Crystals, beloveds, as gifts from God, Source, your Provider, are gifted to you to support and assist in many ways in your lives, and one of these is within your home, office or other building.

As crystals hold the Divine Plan, the Divine Blueprint within them, they are radiating this intention, and energy, at all times so placing any crystal in any position will have a beneficial effect within your environment.

As your vibrations raise, so too does this create a realignment with the crystal energies who can adapt their energetic being to resonate with the inhabitants. Too high a resonance from the crystal could create imbalance within the relationship of guardian and crystal, and this would not be harmonious to either. As the human energies clear from miscreations, and consciousness raises, the crystal being can raise their energy in line with this, creating a new higher level of consciousness, and thus a new level of harmonic relationship is reached.

In this way, a visitor to a house of high vibrational crystals may feel uncomfortable for reasons they cannot understand, and likewise a higher vibrational person may feel a dissonance in an environment where crystals are not looked after appropriately, and are vibrating at a lower level to be a match for the current guardian.

crystals add light and beauty to a home

Crystals add light and beauty to a home; they draw attention to their physical form and create joy, lightness, pleasure, and strengthen the energetic connection between human beings, and Mother Earth who provided the environment for their creation, and evolution.

They bring light by reflecting and absorbing sunlight creating rainbows and colourful dances of light, again bringing fun and pleasure to the environment.

Crystals are known for their protective element and can be programmed to protect from emissions from modern technology, microwave ovens, and so on. They can also be placed outside of the home and programmed to protect the environment and building, and to allow in only the energies of the highest and greatest good, and radiant light.

Crystals placed in the soil will bring in more light and love to the garden, and therefore the whole of your environment, and in addition assist Mother Earth as the light from the sun and moon will be drawn into the crystal and radiate into Mother Earth. A lovingly programmed crystal or crystals placed in the soil will add harmony, love and light with the addition of sharing your intention to support, and express gratitude to, Mother Earth for all that she provides for you.

crystals can bring peace to your home

It expresses understanding, a consciousness if you will, of your sense of oneness, of unity with All That Is and your willingness to work on a higher level to support nature, Mother Earth and the oneness of All That Is, and our ability to be part of this nurturing and harmonising of all things. It supports and radiates light to the soil, the plants, and all living beings in the garden.

Crystals can be decorative and still work their magic in lifting the energies of a room, if for example there is a corner with not much light, a crystal placed here will add light and love and draw attention to its beauty, and create a delightful addition to a room.

Crystals can bring peace to an environment in a gentle and subtle way and this could be useful if there has been any dispute say between neighbours or an upsetting incident within the environment. Programmed to bring peace, and positioned appropriately, the crystal energies can radiate peace to support clearing the energies, and creating harmony once again.

Just looking at a crystal and seeing its beauty, the reflection of light, its shape and form and knowing that it is a gift from God for your benefit and support in this lifetime lifts the spirits and lightens the heart. This heartfelt connection of inner knowingness and the connection to Mother Earth and All that Is, enables crystals to be a creative part in the overall Blueprint for earth and the creation and bringing forth of Nova Earth – a time of love, peace and harmony for all humanity at this special time on earth beloveds.

With our love and gratitude to all crystal beings, Amen.

The Crystal Maze

Beloveds, the Crystal Maze exists in your dimension as a structure of light and love, and holds the energies of the Blueprint for earth, and humanity, and all living beings.

The length of time that humanity has existed on earth is so relatively short compared to the overall existence of your planet, and the universe, and yet in that time has impacted on the earth so dramatically.

Prior to man's existence the earth was self-regulatory, it was organic in the sense of its ability to change and adapt. The earth has her own agenda, if you like, her own journey and was on this path over her existence.

regulating the universe

Earth plates moved, animals appeared and changed, adapted and became extinct, oceans appeared, rivers, streams, mountains, valleys, trees, all of this continued without human interference. Nature evolved, climates changed, landmasses changed, animals roamed the earth in alignment with the climate, and their needs.

Without humanity planet earth would continue to evolve, climates change, landmass movements, mountains, volcanoes, animal species, orbital path, and inner and outer surface of the earth would continue in all its glory.

And this did not, nor would it, continue in isolation without humanity. The crystals inside the earth radiate their energy; this links along ley-lines, it connects to the stars and galactic formations, and to the crystalline grid. And all of this regulates the universe and beyond.

There are many aspects not yet understood by humanity which balance the universal energies although more is being revealed all the time, and as humanity becomes more aware of the possibility of life on other planets (although by the time of publication contact with universal friendly organisations may well have been made), this will completely alter humanity's perception of life in the universe.

Can you begin to see this picture of oneness on a bigger scale, of the vastness of the connections established which maintain the flow of the universe and beyond? And can you see how small a time humanity has been a part of that on earth?

The solar system is always changing

Mother Earth beloveds, has shown through earthquakes, floods, storms and so on especially in 2017, that she is clearing herself, cleansing all that prevents her ascension, prevents her fully stepping into the next stage of her evolution, for herself, and her role within the solar system, and the universal energies and beyond.

She cannot hold back and wait for humanity, she will complete her ascension as part of the ongoing changes all round. For nothing happens in isolation, nothing happens without a cause and a reason. The solar system is always changing and adapting; solar flares occur, energies change constantly to maintain the balance and move forward as their own role in the Blueprint changes so that all forms of life, all sparks of God's love, change and adapt within the Blueprint of God's Divine Plan.

And so within this picture, all is in a constant state of flux

As Mother Earth moves forward, as humanity raises its consciousness in alignment with the Divine Plan, then the Crystal Maze reacts to the changes, increases the light radiant, the knowledge and wisdom, and strengthens connections along ley-lines and with the crystalline grid, and so the connection within the solar system, and within the universe.

And so it is, beloveds, and so it is.

Humanity's ascension is a part of this balance within the universe, and for those who choose to move forwards, life will change to the desired way of equality, fairness, inclusivity, joy, justice, peace, and love for all beings in balance with all living beings, and your home and provider Mother Earth.

And so it is beloveds, and so it is Amen.

We wish you all well on this journey for those who have chosen this path, and see this beautiful new life of radiant joy, creativity, expansion, harmony, fulfilment based on love, respect, gratitude, and appreciation for all that this life offers you as part of the overall Blueprint for life on earth.

And so it is. Amen.

Loving Your Crystals

Crystals, beloveds are so much more than the colourful or clear pieces of rock that you see. The light that radiates from them is immense, and can increase with each loving thought you send to it. For all is energy, all is oneness, and all is part of the omniverse, and God's love for you all.

For all that is created by the Prime Creator, or Source, is provided for all souls, all beings to enjoy and benefit from. They are encoded with light and love, and this can be made available to each soul as that soul awakens in this lifetime to all that is available to them.

See your crystal as a living being, for indeed it is a living being, and one of God's creations for you. Tuning into your crystal and sending it loving thoughts, handling it with love and being grateful for the opportunity to connect, and work with it, will increase its love quotient. In turn as this love energy increases it will add and radiate increased love energies into your home or other environment where they are placed. They can light up dark corners, lift the energy of places with stuck or stagnant energies, and bring in light and love to those who are in need of refreshment.

being of service

Increasing the love energy of your crystal will also strengthen the connection with your own crystalline energy, and lift your energies, and support your releasing and cleansing process of all that no longer serves you. This is an easy way to support you on your path to enlightenment as by sitting with, or tuning into your crystal, you can use the connection to gently let go, and clear, all that prevents you from being the best you can be.

In this way crystals help souls to be in service to the community and beyond, by raising the energies and radiating the light and love, so any increase in your crystals' love quotient will help your surrounding area by radiating this light and increasing the light and love, so raising the overall energies of all souls, all living beings, and Mother Earth, and nature, so as part of service work they play a valuable role.

The increase in light and love also aids the release of wisdoms, knowledge and information stored within the crystals so that this too can be released, and made available, in subtle energetic ways increasing the resonance for all those who wish to tune in and receive.

So beloveds, see what a gift these crystals are not only to yourself, but to all souls, all living beings, and Mother Earth, plants, trees and so on.

blessing the water

Crystals placed in water jugs can be programmed to clear the water, or a simple blessing will clear, cleanse and change the water you drink. Again in blessing the water, you are showing gratitude for all that is being made available to you; the water to sustain you, and the part that water has in the oneness of all things.

By blessing the water you charge the crystal to radiate more light and love, and to drink the water connects you to all waters throughout the world so you are in effect connecting to all waters, showing gratitude and sharing the light and love through this.

Drinking the water connects to your crystalline essence increasing your radiance and strengthening your connection to All That Is.

It connects all souls through blessing, through the crystal energies, and the intention of love and gratitude, the gift from Source, the connection to Mother Earth who allowed the growth of crystals within her being, and the connection to all waters upon your earth. So again can you see beloveds, how one simple act of using a crystal in your water and blessing that crystal, and water, can have an immense impact on the world around you? And we thank you for joining in this simple yet powerful action as part of the overall raising of energies for the creation of Nova Earth.

Crystals can be kept in a small bowl of water to continuously make that connection with waters around the world. Bless the crystals, bless the water, and ask for all waters to be cleared and cleansed and receive the love and light from the crystals to raise the energies of all waters around the world.

Choose your crystals carefully for this purpose, or allow them to choose themselves, and know that each time you see or think of this beautiful creation, you are sending love and light radiating throughout all waters around the world in the most beautiful way, helping to clear and cleanse and bring in the love and light of God your provider, and linking to all crystals within and without the earth to raise the energies for all humanity as part of the creation of Nova Earth, and we thank you for this beautiful act of generosity, appreciation and soul centred love for all.

be creative with your crystals

Enjoy your creations, add flowers if you like, add special symbols if you like, be as creative as you like and share photos of your creations to inspire others to do likewise, and to share more joy and happiness, make people smile and strengthen that connection to all That Is.

And so beloveds, we leave you for this time, we leave you to play and be creative with your crystals, and to know that you are being of the greatest service to all in your own unique way. We love you, we thank you, we honour you, blessings of love and light until next time adieu.

INVOCATION

With this crystal I bring in the light and love of God, Source, the Great Provider so that it may radiate through this crystal into the water and thus connect to all waters around the world.

I bless this water that it may connect through this crystal to all streams, rivers, seas, oceans around this planet and clear and cleanse all that is not for the highest and greatest good of all.

And in this way the crystal energies of love, the wisdoms encoded in the crystals will be released and connect with all waters on this planet and beyond, bringing clarity, enlightenment, purity, to all souls who drink or connect with the waters of the world, that the crystal energies link to the crystals within Mother Earth, and strengthen their connection.

That the crystal energies link to the crystalline essence of all souls, and to the crystalline grid so that all may radiate at the perfect level of joy, love and peace for the highest and greatest good of all, and so be it, and so be it, and so be it, and it is done. Amen.

The Significant Role of the Crystalline Grid

Your world is comprised of many crystalline grids as crystals, in their physical form, are present in multiple places within the universe, your Mother Earth, your physical beings, and beyond, and consequently the role they play in regulating and adapting to the rise in consciousness is of vital importance.

As has been said before, crystals are living beings with a purpose, a plan, and a self regulatory ability alongside a connection to all living beings, Mother Earth, humanity and the universal energies, and thus they form part of the physical structure of the universe within the omniverse.

And all this is part of the Divine Plan so thoughtfully laid down from eons of time ago. For if consciousness is to expand to a 5th dimensional level, there must needs be a structure to hold these energies in place, to connect all matter and manner of things in order to make a cohesive whole, and to be constantly adaptable to the variant changes. For chaos could ensue if humanity began to raise their energies in a constant flow and flux and there was not a structure to hold this in place and maintain a level of stability.

maintaining balance and stability

The level of change and adaptation within each human being is constantly changing and adapting to internal and external forces. Meditations, inner work, connecting to like minded souls, expanding awareness of the global changes towards a more sustainable, ethical world, all raise your internal vibration, and at the same time, outer influences like pollution and negative energies from lower vibrations, toxins from food sources, or energetic mismatches with other humans can all lower your vibrational rate, added to this the erratic weather conditions of storms, floods and so on, and the influx of new energies granted at appropriate times, all affect your crystalline vibrational rate and therefore your connection to the crystals within and without the earth, and in the crystalline grid.

So the importance of this structure to maintain balance and stability during this time of fluctuation and expansion is apparent. The grid connects to the multiverse as the earth does not exist in isolation, and the role and stability of Mother Earth play a vital part in the balance of the whole, so the crystalline grid is a regulatory factor between Mother Earth and beyond.

enjoy the journey

As the crystalline grid energies rise in alignment with the Divine Plan, then humanity continues to evolve towards a 5th dimensional way of being, individually and collectively, and each person has the opportunity to fulfil their soul mission, their path and purpose in this lifetime.

And Mother Earth is on her own path towards ascension, and in coming together energetically with humanity and all living beings, will create a radiant light as part of the whole, and life on earth will be peaceful, radiant, joyful and harmonious.

And this, beloveds, is the Divine Plan as set out, and the crystal resonance of all beings, and Mother Earth, is playing its part in the unfolding of this magnificent plan.

Enjoy the unfoldment, enjoy the journey, and we thank you all for your endeavours in your part in the fulfilment of this Blueprint for life on earth and beyond.

Amen beloveds Amen.

The New Energies have Begun

Beloveds, your awareness of the power and glory of crystals is growing immensely and at all times your crystalline essence is expanding and raising in energetic level. As this occurs your physical body is receiving the benefit of these energies, and the wisdom, and knowledge held in your essence filters out so that what you inherently know without consciously knowing becomes more into your consciousness. And this can be triggered by hearing or reading or seeing something that you suddenly click with and think – well yes I know that but did not know I knew it but it makes sense and feels right.

For you are all born with so much knowledge and agree to put this aside as you enter your earth physicality, and your journey on earth reignites this knowledge at the appropriate time for you to become consciously aware of.

The fact that your crystalline essence and DNA already hold this information makes the transition of information to conscious awareness subtle and safe for you, for you cannot adapt to too much information at once, it must needs be integrated into your awareness at an appropriate rate for you to absorb. Then as you look at the world you think, well yes, this is how the earth operates, this is how nature works, this is further evidence that we all need to work together in unity consciousness for the highest and greatest good of all because we are all interlinked and interdependent.

And thus you build on this knowledge and awareness as you clear more of that which no longer serves you and that which holds you back from being the most magnificent being of light you can be.

In turn your light quotient increases and your light assists those around you; it makes your life flow more easily, and it enhances your enjoyment and understanding of life. In turn this adds to the overall energy of the crystalline grid which then radiates at a higher rate for the earth, and all living beings, and benefits all of these plus the outer energies beyond your orbit.

changes in attitude and perspective

And so again this shows the beauty of the overall plan for you on earth, the creation of structures within you, and within your universe, to allow this expansion, growth in awareness, call it what you will, to occur on so many levels and to be held within the crystalline grid structure for the benefit of all.

Because your DNA changes and your crystalline essence changes, the next generation of children will be born with this already in their system so that they are more awake and aware and see the world from a different perspective, and this is being borne out by the changes in attitude and approach to education – where the current system is not a good match for the new energies, and in the examples of young people who set up initiatives to help those in need of food, housing and general support. They see the need and are prepared to take action to improve a person's life or help Mother Earth through clearing litter or other initiatives. They are awake to the needs of Mother Earth and to humanity, and find ways to support this.

Meditation is being taught in schools as a means of being in touch with their inner peace and giving them life skills which previous generations did not have access to.

momentum for change

So the momentum for change gathers apace with the new generations, whose light and energies will in turn raise the energies for the next generation, and so on, and so on with each generation being born not knowing anything different and building on the energies of compassion, love, equality, fairness, diversity, justice, peace, love and harmony, and so it will continue.

As Mother Earth continues to clear and cleanse and raise her energies, the interplay between the crystals within her being and those of humanity's crystalline essence, will continue to raise energies, raise awareness, and build a stronger link between humanity and the world around increasing respect for all aspects of life.

Thus the importance and relevance of crystals, and our crystalline essence, becomes more apparent as our awareness grows of the amazing gifts available to humanity, and the continuation of growth, and expansion becomes a reality.

The new energies have begun, are held in the crystalline structures, and will continue to grow and expand in Divine timing as part of the Divine Plan for all on earth.

Sit with these thoughts and allow the information to permeate your being in the light and love of God. Amen.

Creating Nova Earth

Dear beloveds, we happily share more news today for this insightful book about the wonders of crystals; for happiness is an important aspect of the reason for crystals' existence, and their role for humanity.

Looking at a crystal always raises the spirits as they are such beautiful, colourful, amazingly formed beings so that alone raises the vibration of all who look at them.

Then having them in your home raises your resonance by the energy they emit, and the beauty of their being and presence in a room.

Wearing crystals as jewellery brings joy and happiness, and raises your vibration by working with your energies. They also give joy to others who can see the jewellery you are wearing, and may comment on it.

Wearing as a talisman, or keeping in your pocket, a specially programmed crystal brings you joy for its very presence, reassurance, and confidence, and the joy of knowing it is working with you.

Working with crystals for healing purposes brings joy as you intuit which crystals to use, and the joy of knowing you are supporting your own, or another's journey to wellbeing.

Using crystals in grids to support ongoing healing for Mother Earth or other purposes brings joy as you feel the gratitude of being able to use these gifts of God to share love, healing and Divine energy and intention towards peace for all on earth, or whichever purposes and intention you have created your grid.

And these are some of the ways in which crystals bring joy into your life at this time.

And the creation of joy and happiness adds to your wellbeing, raises your energies, and your crystalline essence. As all beings are linked through their crystalline essence, and through their connection to the crystals within Mother Earth, then this raises the vibration for all. In turn this raises the energy of the crystalline grid, and again as all are linked to this crystalline grid then all are affected by a raise in energies.

And so the joy and happiness created by looking at a crystal has a far bigger effect and impact than you can realise in the bigger picture, and helps to raise the energies for all.

And it is this continuous raising of energies over time which has enabled humanity to pass the point of no return, a point of creating the new energies for all, creating the opportunity for Nova Earth. And this will be a time of creativity, as the mind becomes less dominant, and intuition and inner guidance become more prominent with heart-centred actions and unity consciousness.

creating unity consciousness

In describing how we are all linked through our crystalline essence, and the crystals in the earth, and the crystalline grid, you can envisage how unity consciousness evolves through raising the energies to a point where people 'get' our connectivity, and understand that all actions affect all people, and Mother Earth, and beyond, and so a judgement made and spoken that is not in alignment with the highest and greatest good for all can adversely affect the overall energetic level, whereas a kind word or thoughtful action raises the energy for all. And in this way inner peace evolves, judgements decrease, separation and isolation dissolve and awareness of creating heart-centred, responsible thoughts and actions for all aspects of life become more prevalent for all souls.

As people's intuition increases, they will become more in touch with the energies, awareness and knowledge of earlier times, of ancestors where this was a way of life, consideration to all aspects of life on earth, before personal gain, greed, accumulation and disrespect for other forms of life developed.

And so in creating these joyful energies and assisting in raising the overall energetic level, you are assisting in the total ability to create unity consciousness and thus peace on earth, peace for all beings, and Mother Earth, a life of joy, happiness, creativity, expansion, harmony, inclusivity, equality and love; love for all, love for self, and love for All That Is.

And we joyously thank crystals for the role they play in this creation of Nova Earth as part of the Divine Plan created, and laid out, and offered to all humanity for the highest and greatest good of all.

We joyously celebrate these gifts of God. Amen.

Crystals hold the Vibrational Essence of Humanity's Desire to Reshape the World

Crystals hold the record, and the essence, of All That Is across all times, levels and dimensions. The record of the earth is within them, the movements, the changes, the oceans, the temperature changes, movements of mountains, and so on, are all recorded back to the beginning of what you call time.

Along with this the changing continents, the civilizations, the energies of those civilizations, the human aspect, the animal kingdom, and nature forms are all recorded.

And you may ask how all this can be recorded in a crystal, in a compact form that is part of the earth. In the same way you may wonder how a silicon chip can create so much and be so effective when so small. And why does this happen, why is all history stored for all times, levels and dimensions?

Crystals are part of the earth; they are formed as the earth forms, and encapsulate all of the energies of the Divine Plan and Blueprint for earth.

They are gifts from God, determined at the time of creation to be of service to Mother Earth, humanity, all living beings, and as part of the universe. They are extremely complex forms designed to be eternally of service.

Humans have a crystalline essence, and there is a crystalline grid around the planet, all things of crystalline form are linked and united on a vibrational level, and communicate as such.

Therefore, when the energies of humanity raise collectively and individually, then the energies of the crystalline grid raise, and this is part of the evolution of life on earth, and the co-creation of Nova Earth as pre-ordained eons of time ago.

The crystals hold all the wisdom and knowledge of the earth and humanity, and raising the vibration allows more wisdoms and knowledge to be released at the appropriate time. Thus this wonderful interplay of vibrational connections between all things crystalline, supports the clearing of the old stagnant energies, and the blossoming of new lighter, brighter energies for the highest and greatest good of all.

fulfilment of the Divine Plan for all

As life on earth unfolds, as the DNA of human beings changes and is more fully utilised, as changes in perception, attitudes, approach to life and governance move forward, so the evidence of the progress being made in all areas becomes evident.

This encourages those just awakening that change for the better is happening, and confirms for those on this path, that more and more exciting developments are unfolding in the glory of the Divine Plan.

Humanity can begin to visualise how they wish the world to be, how they wish to see their community running, how they wish to see peace for all, equality, inclusivity, sustainability, zero waste, relevant and appropriate education, housing for all, and so on, and so on.

And all these energies and intentions will be stored within the crystals to hold and maintain the vibrational essence of humanity's desire to reshape the world, and for the fulfilment of the Divine Plan for all.

The amazing gift of crystals knows no bounds, and resounds in the love of God, world without end. Amen.

Crystal Blessings

Crystals have many functions as we have shared before, they bring in the light, the love of God, and they connect you to Mother Earth in many ways known and unknown, seen and unseen, understood and not understood.

They are decorative, add joy to your rooms, assist in bringing balance and harmony to your physicality, and are used in technology, in your computers, and many other areas of technology.

And we ask, are there many other objects which can bring so much joy, so much lightness, be so beneficial in so many ways to your lives as these crystal beings? And this is not to mention the storing of wisdom and information within their beingness which is magnificent and fascinating, and this is the area of crystal beingness we wish to share in this insight.

For crystals hold all the knowledge of the formation of the earth, they hold all the energies of the changes that have taken place over millions of years as the earth plates have moved and temperatures have changed, as mountains formed, ice melted, and waters froze, and eventually as civilizations existed on earth, all the energetic changes that occurred from the influence of mankind.

And so in this way, humanity is linked to the crystal energy in ways which are inseparable, and this continues in the present day, as changes continue to occur so these too are recorded.

As humanity evolves, and as consciousness awakens, so your crystalline essence changes, your DNA changes, your whole essence changes, and this too is related to the crystal beings.

As humanity awakens, and the energies of the crystalline grid raise, so this also affects the crystal beings; as all is one, and inter-related and inter-dependent, so this crystal essence connects all aspects of life and is continuously adjusting.

As Mother Earth changes, evolves, adapts, cleanses so the changes are stored and relate to the crystal beingness, the record keepers, if you like of life on earth.

The crystals inside of earth adapt, store and resonate on a new level, and they also relate and resonate with those on the outer plane of earth and beyond, and so all is in a constant state of adjustment in alignment with the new energies, and with the evolution of humanity as part of the Divine Plan for all.

Is this not a magnificent concept, a magnificent gift to humanity that you may hold a piece of crystal, however small, in your hand and know that it is connected on so many levels to the world around you, and to your own physical being?

Within the hologram in the centre of the earth special crystals are arranged to be the record keepers of life on earth. Some of these relate to humanity and they maintain the records of each of your lives. As you are born into this world a mark is made to denote a new life cycle here on earth, and as your physical body and soul separate at the end of this life cycle, so an energetic resonance is added to the marker to record your experiences in this life time, and more of this will be shared in later insights.

love for all humanity

For now suffice to say that as humanity evolves, and consciousness raises, so the energetic imprint from each life raises in accordance, and this assists in raising the overall resonance on this planet, and that of the crystalline grid.

Should you decide to return to this planet, your resonance will be raised in accordance with your previous existence, and your awareness will be higher.

Increasingly souls are being born remembering more, and with a greater awareness, and higher consciousness because the overall resonance is raising.

And so the Divine Plan unfolds in all its glory, with all the gifts given to you from the start of time, and continues as consciousness raises towards creating Nova Earth; a life of peace, equality, harmony, justice for all, and love for all humanity.

We bid you farewell until time again beloveds, crystal blessings to you all.

Crystals and the Wheel of Life

Our next insight concerns the Lemurians, and their connection to crystals, and to the Wheel of Life. The Wheel of Life (although it will appear under different titles in different situations) relates to the history and knowledge passed down through generations and originates from the Pleiadian Starseeds who seeded the earth. The Pleiadian Starseeds transferred this wisdom so that the Lemurians could benefit from, and enjoy, the beauty of the connection with all things.

For although this was learning in the sense that children at school today learn, it was presented in a totally different way to the children to be meaningful, relevant, a part of their lineage, and a joy to integrate into their daily lives in an ongoing way.

Parents (mothers directly) were involved in this process, and communities were all a part of this evolution to maintain the balance as an individual, community, and with Mother Earth, and all living beings, and the universe.

And so you may ask where do crystals come into this beautiful process? Well beloveds, crystals hold all the wisdoms and knowledge from the start of the formation of earth so as the Pleiadians seeded life, so the crystals began to form and hold all the history of all things, and so they acted as record keepers, and were held in great reverence by the Lemurians.

meditating with crystals

Around the Wheel of Life with its 5 spokes and the central sun in the centre, crystals were used in conjunction with the teachings received by children. This gave them a greater connection to their lineage knowing that the crystals held the connection to their forefathers and to Mother Earth, knowing how wonderful it was to have these gifts from God connecting them energetically to the planet which provided them with food, shelter, beauty, and offered the opportunity for a physical life on this planet.

So they held the crystals in great reverence and gratitude and connected with them during these times of education.

In addition to the spoken teachings they could meditate with the crystals to seek answers to their personal queries. The community as a whole could also meditate with them if they desired information, and confirmation, on a community issue to act for the highest and greatest good of all.

crystal layouts

As crystals hold all the wisdoms, they would continue to receive energies from each generation which could be accessed in the future, and this method was used in gratitude and respect as part of their overall desire to remain in harmony with all things.

Crystal layouts were used at certain times of the year as described in an earlier insight (see Ceremony to Honour Mother Earth), and celebrations to cleanse and honour the crystals themselves were regularly held.

The crystals used also linked to the crystals holding the Akashic record for each soul so that the life purpose of each soul could be connected to; this would help the individual to maintain their purpose and path in that lifetime.

More information on the Wheel of Life can be found on www.thewayofpeace-lindsayball.co.uk in Teachings from Lemuria.

security and freedom

Young children up to the age of 6/7, when they began the introduction formally to the Wheel of Life, connected with crystals for meditation and ceremonies, and understood their relevance to the Lemurian life and their connection to Mother Earth. And from this they intuitively turned to crystals during this time. They also saw how important these were as part of their heritage, and grew up respecting and being grateful, for these gifts.

In all, in this way, they had many resources to support their development, and as the community acted as one in its desire to remain harmonious within itself, with Mother Earth and all living beings, they were freely able to receive guidance from other members of the community, draw strength from the lineage and wisdoms passed down, and from the crystals which were part of their lives.

This provided a security and freedom within clear aspirations which enabled them to flourish and evolve as light beings enjoying life on planet earth.

Amen beloveds, amen.

Crystals Hold the Energies of the Blueprint for Earth

Crystals appear for many reasons, as keepers of information and wisdom of long held insights, and energies of the Blueprint for earth, the Divine Plan for all.

As has been said before, the Blueprint, the Divine Plan was laid out many moons ago so that the potential to achieve peace on earth, and to move into Nova Earth, was established.

These many times since this precept have all been a move towards creating peace; a life of joy, balance, harmony, equality and fulfilment on earth. A time for souls to experience a physical life on earth, and to connect with Mother Earth who allowed for this creation.

For had the Blueprint not been laid down, had a Divine Plan not been instigated, then we would not now be able to communicate that 2012 was a significant marker, and this marker has been crossed, and humanity and Mother Earth are now moving towards the creation of a 5th dimensional life, and Nova Gaia.

Previous civilizations have existed which have provided different lifestyles on this planet where souls came to experience that lifestyle within that time. These civilisations progressed but ultimately did not continue due to not being in alignment with the Divine Plan, and destruction on earth caused the downfall and ultimate demise of these civilisations, and in Lemurian times the energy dissipated and souls were not drawn to continue in this plane of experience.

changes are being witnessed

However, the crystals have always been there, have always held the Blueprint, and have always held the wisdoms and knowledge, and this holds true today.

As humanity raises its energies, its crystalline essence and its crystalline grid, so too do the crystals begin to release more energetic intentions in alignment with the Divine Plan. Those who resonate with this energy will integrate these energies physically and spiritually, and so continue the cycle of raising the vibration for all.

As you all breathe the same air, as you all drink the same water, so the resonance of this awareness is passed unconsciously from person to person, and so the wisdoms are absorbed by humanity on many levels. For those who work intuitively, or consciously connect to their inner knowing, this absorption aids their connection to the wisdoms of All That Is and assists in their decision making, conscious awareness, and way of life.

Many changes are being witnessed on earth, and many of these are due to the commitment of souls who are fulfilling their soul mission to raise the overall energies, share their skills and co-create Nova Earth.

This diligence supports the changes being witnessed as the overall energies raise, as people tune into their own intuition, as they begin to sense the need for change, to work with Mother Earth, to work together as one, to work together in equality, fairness, respect, love and harmony.

humanity's awakening

As light workers raise and hold the energy this radiates out for the benefit of all, and while not all souls will awaken in this lifetime, it creates the opportunity for more souls to awaken and make the necessary changes. It also creates the foundation for the next generations who are being born with higher awareness and energies so they quickly establish themselves as innovators, energy workers, healers, conscious decision makers, and new light beings continuing the creation of Nova Earth.

And in this way crystals will continue to release wisdoms, and intelligence, to support this co-creation of peace on earth and manifest the Blueprint, and Divine Plan, for all.

We thank the crystal kingdom for being on earth at this time to hold the energies of the Divine Plan, and for their work in releasing energies, and wisdoms, at the appropriate time supporting humanity's awakening and raising the resonance for all.

And in this way, working on many levels, the prophesied time of peace will evolve over all times, levels and dimensions, world without end. Amen.

The Balance of Life on Earth

Dear beloveds it is our joy, as always, to celebrate the progress being made in your world, and to see the consciousness of humanity opening and growing in the new energies.

And this has been occurring over many generations and lifetimes for those who came here to begin this process for humanity, and Mother Earth, at this time.

As we know, all is planned; all is laid out in the Divine Plan although the actual timing and manifestation is within the power, and creation, of humanity. The more souls awaken, and the more who become aware, the greater the momentum to advance and move into the new energies.

In a cyclical manner this in turn raises the energies of the crystalline grid which holds the awakening consciousness of humanity, and holds the energies, and radiates these out to support the awakening of other souls.

In this delightful way, each act of kindness, compassion, positive thought, new concept to help others and the planet, each act and word in love, and joy, increases the radiance of this grid.

be love

Thus its light energies radiate even brighter. So every time you perform an act of kindness, speak words of love, move into heart-centred compassion and understanding, each action to support the planet and all living beings adds to your radiance, and that of all others.

Be love, be compassion, be the energy you wish to see radiating throughout the universe, and feel the benevolence of your actions, thoughts and deeds to this process of ascension.

The crystalline grid continues to grow and expand although in some areas it is stronger and more impactful than others, but overall the radiance reaches all parts of the world, and the universe.

Again it is the crystal ability to change, adapt and hold the new energies which enables this constant upgrading to occur, for crystals can hold the energy and intention from heart-centred words, deeds, thoughts and actions, and this ability to then radiate out these energies is due to the generosity of the crystals, and Mother Earth, who work in conjunction with all things crystal to uphold this grid, for Mother Earth allows for the creation of the crystals within her which connect with the crystalline grid and create this magnificent record for the benefit of all.

crystal technology

Crystal technology will become more widely accepted; it is already an integral part of many technologies used today, and as science and technology advance the qualities of crystals will be greatly used to advance many aspects of your life, and assist in cleaning the environment, and providing cleaner air, and renewable technologies which will reduce the need to use the ever depleting resources of Mother Earth, and allow her to heal the wounds of actions of mankind in removing, without consent or consideration, vast areas and amounts of her very being in order to create goods which then in turn pollute and mar her energies and well-being.

changes in attitude

And crystals will help in adjusting this activity in providing alternative energy sources and supplies which will not pollute or create imbalance within this awesome planet who is your home, your shelter and provider, and who by Universal Law, must needs be honoured, protected, thanked and revered for her own being, her ascension, and her generosity in allowing humanity to experience life in a physical form in such a beautiful situation.

Changes in attitude, awareness, and activity are beginning to emerge, and humanity is responding well to these changes. Individuals are creating systems, and tools, to repair the damage and pollution to the waters and general awareness of the need to attend to, and respect Mother Earth, are emerging.

As these energies grow so too does the energy of the crystalline grid, and so the circle continues to emerge, and grow for the benefit of all. As this awakening continues the benefits to all will emerge, and the balance of life on earth will return to its Blueprint, and peace will reign supreme on earth.

Adieu beloveds, adieu till time again.

A Myriad Ways to Work with Crystal Energies

Our sharing of wisdoms and insights, on all things crystal, is so that you can understand and tune into the full magnificence of crystals, and how they may assist you in your lives.

And this could be your general awareness; it could be for use in grids that you are drawn to create, for using them in healings, for your own benefit, and that of others.

Or you may choose to support Mother Earth using crystals; use them in meditations and manifestations, tune into them where they are in the earth or just to enjoy their beauty and form.

Whichever way or ways you decide to use crystals they are delighted to be of service, and to share their wisdoms and knowledge, which they have carried forward to this auspicious time.

Their beauty and form attract people all over the world whether they are consciously awakening or not, and help raise the energies of the crystalline grid, and your own crystalline essence, in an ongoing way.

As time has no real meaning, or relevance, the crystals just 'are', and so their very beingness is working to spread the love and light of God for all times, across all levels, and dimensions.

And so if you choose to carry a crystal in your pocket you are benefitting from its energies and may dedicate it to a certain desire, or allow it to work its magic generally, for the highest and greatest good of all.

dedicating your crystal

If you choose to form a grid of crystals, it can be dedicated for a purpose, formed on a map of the world if you wish to dedicate it to creating peace on earth, it can be used in water to assist in creating beautiful crystals in the water when blessed with love and positive energies.

It can be dedicated to a certain project you have in mind. Perhaps you are thinking of moving house so the crystal may be dedicated to finding the house most in alignment with your highest and greatest good, and if there is a particular house you wish to buy it can be placed on a photograph of this house, if this house is in alignment with your greatest good.

Crystals can be placed on any photograph, it could be of a garden, a building, a town or a city where you wish to send light and love, in dedicating the crystal to that cause you are radiating light and love to that image.

You may choose to wear crystal jewellery so that you can see its beauty, and others benefit too, along with the benefits of any properties the crystal may radiate out.

crystal skulls

You may wish to buy a crystal in the form of a crystal skull, and this brings a whole new dimension to the crystal world.

There are many well-known crystal skulls throughout the world with many mysteries to them which make fascinating reading. The Mitchell-Hedges skull, Rainbow, Max, ET, AMAR are to name but a few, some ancient and some more recent.

Modern skulls are available in many forms, and sizes, and have a multitude of uses. The ancient skulls hold much wisdom and much research has been carried out and written about, and they often travel the world with their guardians working with different groups, in different areas, raising the energies and releasing the older stuck energies which are no longer relevant in the new energies.

Crystal skulls can be worn as jewellery, carried in your pocket, used in meditation, grids and transformational work.

They are so formed so that we identify with their physiology, and can be seen as a friendly energy, we can identify with. Formed in this shape the energies are magnified over a non-skull crystal and so are more powerful to work with.

As with all crystals when you allow your intuition to guide you, the crystal or crystal skull will choose you, and once you have bought or been gifted the skull, a name will often present itself to you.

When our partner in channelling Lindsay, first bought her crystal skull the name Charlie came through, and as she worked with this energy a personality developed and communications evolved.

Subsequent skulls have named themselves Goldie, Susannah, Hope, George, Starlite, and Mission for Peace, and we form this collective who now communicate as The Crystal Team, and are so delighted to share with you insights and wisdoms to assist you on your journey.

We leave you here for today and look forward to sharing our next insights and further information on crystal skulls, and so till then beloveds, blessings of love and peace to you all, Amen.

All Souls will Walk in the Love and Light of God to Bring Peace on Earth

Dear beloveds, we share with you today how crystal consciousness will help transform the world into the new energies so that Nova Earth will be created for the benefit of all.

And by all we do indeed mean all, all humanity, all living beings, all aspects of Mother Earth from her waters, to the soil, to the mountains, and so on. It includes the relationship to the other planets in your solar system, and with this to the outer reaches of the universe, for all is connected, and all is one, so changes to one aspect affect all others.

As the crystalline grid raises its energies, as the crystals inside Mother Earth raise theirs, as the crystals holding the Akashic records adapt, as the crystalline essence in the human body raises, then so too does the crystalline resonance change for all.

The constant changing and raising of all positive energies, of all releasing of old stagnant energies, the sending of love and compassion, the meditations for peace, all acts of kindness and support, and many, many other acts help raise the overall energies for all souls.

holding the light

As for those souls who are just awakening, the transition is clearer as the energies are raising in transition too and being held by the countless, tireless, light workers who have agreed to bring in and hold the light in this lifetime.

For there are many aspects at work beloveds; there are those you can see and understand, and those you cannot see, and those as yet unknown to you but much is happening on many levels to support the creation of Nova Earth from behind the scenes, as it were, as this is part of the Divine Plan as laid out eons of time ago.

Light is being sent to earth in alignment with the plan at strategic opportunities, and we watch with delight as each soul awakens to the love and light of God, and to the oneness of All That Is.

As this occurs, the emphasis of the soul's direction begins to awaken to the true path and purpose of their existence and intuition prompts the individual to be guided towards that which is in their highest and greatest good.

positive developments

More notice is taken of items of news showing positive developments around the world to promote equality, fairness, harmony, justice, joy, and good health.

More notice is taken of the news of innovations supporting those in need of support so that they may become independent and live life in fullness and joy.

More notice is taken of news locally of environmental issues, of reducing plastic usage and waste, of energy saving techniques, of community projects bringing people together in a common cause.

More notice is taken of other people also awakening as souls are drawn together in like-minded activities and meditations, in discussion, and meeting up to share all of these updates.

More notice is taken of different approaches to economics, of wealth distribution, of sustainability, of new technology for renewable energy, and as souls awaken to these possibilities they see the possibility for change, they see hope and optimism which in turn both spurs them on to continue on this path, and to raising the energies of the crystalline essence for all.

And so in this way progress is made and continues towards creating peace on earth. The desire for peace is in the hearts and minds of people as they awaken to the possibility, and desire, for peace.

acts of kindness

And so we thank each person for their awakening, for their participation, for every act of kindness, and support, for every thought of love sent to another, for all the compassion for those in need, for all the love and light sent to governments and leaders to support making decisions for the highest and greatest good of all.

And in this way all souls will evolve in their true light whichever way that is, and all souls will walk in the love and light of God to bring peace on earth, and goodwill to all men.

See the crystalline grid shimmering with radiant light, sense your crystalline essence raising in line with this, and releasing all that no longer serves you.

See the crystals within and without the earth radiating the loving essence of God, Source, the Great Provider, call it what you will, and see all humanity at peace, and all living beings at peace, and Mother Earth in her true radiance and beauty.

We thank you beloveds, we honour you and celebrate all your endeavours towards creating Nova Earth as decreed in the Divine Plan. Amen and so it is, thy will be done.

Crystals are Beyond Anything In Their Magnificence

They are beautiful, they are of God, they are energy raisers and balancers, and can be used in a myriad ways to assist humanity in moving forward in their individual and collective evolution, and the creation of Nova Earth.

Crystals can assist in group situations to enhance the effects of meditation when used for a specific purpose, so for example a group of one or more persons can select and bless a crystal, and use it to enhance the energetic intention of the meditation. This could be for peace, for a specific situation say following a natural disaster, to help a specific group of humanity, or other reason or occasion.

It is known and understood that a meditation of one or more persons is more powerful than a single person meditating alone so one or more people, even if not in the same location, can add in the energies of a crystal to bring in even more light and love to the event.

That crystal will connect to all other crystal energies, to the crystals in the centre of the earth, to those outside of the earth, and to those in the crystalline grid, and so all loving intentions and thoughts, will be magnified significantly through all these ways.

co-creating Mother Earth

When you are in a group and choose to use a crystal in this way, see and sense the energies being magnified many-fold and radiating around the world and beyond, connecting to other crystal energies powerfully raising the energies for all.

And these meditations do not need to be of long duration as the new energies are very clear and powerful, and will work in shorter times than previously.

Sense the impact you are creating, and be aware of the impact of your own crystalline essence as part of the oneness of All That Is, as the overall impact supports the ascension process for humanity, and the co-creation of Mother Earth.

In the same way using crystals for grids is equally powerful, and can be a fun, and joyful way to create potent energies for the highest and greatest good. Be guided by your intuition to choose your crystals and how to create the grid. Join with others to create beautiful forms and dedicate them to your chosen theme or dedicate them to the highest and greatest good of all in whichever way is most appropriate for these crystals, as the crystal intelligence will work for that aspiration if invited to do so.

And so in this way joyfully working with crystals, or using crystal skulls in the same way, will bring light and love into your home, your meditation group, your creative grids, and be radiating magnificent energies for all.

Enjoy being creative, enjoy working with your crystals, and celebrate the gifts available to you, to support all humanity, Mother Earth and all living beings at this auspicious time on earth. Adieu beloveds till time again. Amen.

Crystal Skulls helping to Raise Human Consciousness

Crystals, beloveds, come in many forms and can be used in many ways. We have discussed how they can be used as part of a health and well-being programme, to create light and beauty in your home, to wear as jewellery, and in grids, and so on, and as the crystal energies continue to raise so you will be guided to use them in other ways too.

Crystal skulls have been an important part of the crystal world dating back many moons and this is the subject of this insight – although there is so much information to share on this topic that there will be other insights in this book, and in future books, yet to be channelled by our partner here Lindsay.

Why are crystals fashioned into the shape of a head or a skull is an oft asked question, and in answer we reply that it is a form that you are familiar with, a form you identify with and one you could conceivably think of as a friend. In recognising the form, your brain and senses will identify with the familiarity regardless of the size of the skull.

As with all crystals, the form of the crystal in this style will draw your attention, and as with all crystals it will choose you to be its guardian rather than you choosing it.

Once you have taken home this crystal form it will begin the journey of taking on a personality if you work with it, and connect with it. The more you make this connection, the more you will sense its personality and how it wishes to work with you, and its purpose in doing so, and often a name will intuitively come to you for this skull.

sending love to troubled areas

There are many well-known skulls of different ages, and these exhibit energies and personalities which differ greatly, and their purpose for being here differs greatly too. There is much discussion between those who believe in the capabilities of skulls, and those who are not yet awakened to the possibilities and potentialities of these crystal beings.

Crystal skull Susannah, a delightful Rose Quartz skull brings the energies of unconditional love and peace, and she will radiate these energies at trouble spots around the world cooling heated situations, and enfolding all concerned in loving, peaceful energies. She may be considered small in a physical presence but her energy and intention can have a vast impact globally in trouble areas.

Skulls can be worn as jewellery, and will be powerfully working at all times to fulfil the role they chose to come here to perform at this exciting time on earth. Visibly they evoke conversations and interest, and help awaken people by their visible presence.

Crystal skulls can be used on grids, and this brings in a whole new energy over using regular crystal forms as the personality of the skull will come into play and can bring additional fun, lightness, joy, wisdom, and information to the grid.

Crystal skulls can by their very form, become friends, advisors, confidantes, and many souls are attracted to their skulls in this way. After working with them and sensing their personalities it is easy to see how a relationship can evolve as with another human being. In different circumstances a different skull might be a closer option, for example, if you are feeling in need of lightness and joy a particular skull may catch your eye and you know his/her personality is brighter, you will be drawn to work with this one.

raising the energy of all things

On a day when you feel more contemplative you may work with one whose energy/personality is more in tune with your needs in the same way you may ring one human friend for a chat, or another one for a more serious discussion. And in this way the form of the crystal skull works very well to deepen our understanding and relationship with all things crystal which in turn raises the energy of all things, the crystalline grid, and our crystalline essence, and furthers the energy sent around the world through the subtle channels designed for this purpose.

It also links to all the crystal skulls around the world, and information shared between a group or family of skulls, will always be updated when one skull releases information and wisdoms, or when its energies are raised through working with its guardian.

The same applies when skulls are used in healing and rebalancing work. Grids made with intention, meditations using the skulls, and prayers and offerings, resound through a family of skulls in the same way as they do a human family. In this way the human consciousness is raised exponentially towards the critical tipping point towards creating Nova Earth and peace for all as decreed in the Divine Plan, the Blueprint for all.

We honour all crystal skull guardians, and thank all crystal skulls for the invaluable role played in this sharing of information, and wisdom, as part of this plan so that peace may reign supreme on earth.

Thank you beloveds, thank you. Amen.

Crystal Skulls and the Divine Plan

Crystal skulls radiate at a higher frequency than non skull crystals because their form is more concentrated and deliberately created into a form resembling a human head.

The head of a human contains the brain and therefore it is not an unacceptable link to think of the skull as an intelligent form containing experience, knowledge, and wisdom.

This fact that the crystal itself has been around since the beginning of creation, or what you call the beginning of time, (in fact 2 different things altogether), means that it carries all of the changes experienced in the creation of Mother Earth, the temperature changes, geological changes, and so on, means it already is a power house of knowledge. It also contains the Blueprint or Divine Plan as all was created to allow for the unfolding of this plan, and crystals play their part in this.

Therefore the identification of a familiar form containing a storehouse for wisdom and information means the skulls are accepted as such, and added to their personality, means they are very effective beings to work with on any manor of subjects and themes.

Add to this the qualities of the crystal itself; so some may help evolve your intuition, others may help you remain grounded and in balance, others may help you in health and well-being, and so on, and so forth.

Spend time with your skulls, identify their qualities, sit with them, meditate with them, and ask them how they would like to support you in this lifetime.

all souls are connected

For this is the purpose in their personality; for the being to 'drop in', after you have been guided to buy it; the personality is choosing to be with you to support you, to work with you, to help you fulfil your true destiny in this lifetime. Let your soul communicate with that of the crystal being, and allow the intuition to guide you on your next step.

All souls are connected as we are all part of the oneness of All That Is. We all breathe the same air, drink the same water, live on this planet, and so our souls are linked, but they are only part of our total soul existence, and we can reconnect with other aspects of our souls through different means, in order to expand our consciousness and reach our full potential.

As all is energy, the personality of the crystal skulls is energy in a different form, it is all part of God's love in providing so many aspects to support us on earth, at this time, in the creation of peace on earth, Nova Earth, the new Golden Age. And so delight in each form that God sends these gifts, in each form that you may reach out for wisdom, strength, courage, fortitude, faith and love, to work through these times of change to see completion of the Divine Plan for all.

And thus the gifts of God are boundless, and can be incorporated into our everyday lives so that we can choose those that are right for us, and crystal skulls may not be the right path for all, to connect with at the appropriate times.

things come full circle

Your skull will evolve with you and as your consciousness raises, so the crystal skull will release more wisdoms and information, and strengthen its connection to you as you expand in awareness and joy of the potentialities for change, and witness the difference this makes in your life, and to those around you.

As this planet was seeded by the Pleiadians, and as they are still connected to us and with us, the earth's connection to them is lovingly constant. As the crystals form within the earth, so this connection to their Starseeds evolves, and as you work with the crystal skulls this reaffirms your connection with these beings, and your place in the cosmos and the origin of earth.

And so you see things come full circle, and the circle of life continues to evolve, grow and expand in a non-linear way for all, as life on this planet moves towards the time of peace foretold eons of time ago.

And so beloveds enjoy your crystal skulls knowing their timelessness, their origin, their connection to beyond the creation of Mother Earth, and the return to connection with the Pleiadian Starseeds, and know that you are part of all of this, and your connection to the skulls will help assist and guide you in truly magnificent ways beyond your current imaginings, so enjoy your connections to All That Is, and your part in the oneness of All That Is.

Adieu to you beloveds till time again.

Creating Waves of Multidimensional Energy

Dear beloveds we continue on our theme of crystal skulls, and expand on the wisdom and knowledge that can be contained therein.

Many well known skulls are held with their guardians for safe keeping, and many are taken around the world by their guardians to connect with like-minded souls around the world. Some are used in energy balancing being used physically in the earth to link energy lines and portals, and in a distant way in meditations, and higher energy links.

When several guardians arrange to hold a meditation, say for peace, working with the crystal skulls, the energetic intention created is of a higher and greater impact than using crystals, and naturally is higher than just one skull working on its own.

As we have noted, the crystals are from the earth and therefore contain the link with Mother Earth, all that has been, and all that will be is stored in their beingness. This is amplified when created into a skull form, and amplifies the properties of the particular crystal too. The personality of the crystal skull joins in additionally to enhance the process, and so the overall energetic intention is immense.

Each skull has its own purpose, its own intention, its own energy, and this combination adds exponentially to the combined energies of the meditation.

being in balance with All That Is

The crystal skull Susannah, for example, being Rose Quartz has a soft, gentle energy, unconditional love and peace emanate from her being. She brings this energy to any area of imbalance, to calm, to connect souls to the love in their hearts, and reconnect them to their inner knowingness.

Mission for Peace crystal skull carries an immense energetic intention for peace; inner peace within the hearts and minds of all souls, and an expression of outer peace to all souls, all living beings and Mother Earth. The Blueprint is stored and coded within, and this too emanates energetically into any situation to unfold the hearts and minds of all souls to the inner knowingness that there will be peace on earth; there will be kindness and thoughtfulness in place of self-aggrandisement, and there will be equality, fairness, justice and harmony for all souls.

Crystal skull Hope embodies the essence of hope, of fearless optimism, of optimism for humanity's awakening; humanity's awakening to the love of God, to the awakening to the power and intention of peace on earth, and to the awakening of the possibilities and potentialities for all on earth, for all living beings and Mother Earth.

His clarity of crystal qualities brings clarity to the vision of life on earth; a life of harmony, peace, joy and happiness in balance with All That Is, and as decreed in the Blueprint for all.

Crystal skull Charlie has a lightness of energy, and a power of transformation, so he brings lightness and laughter, a bubbling essence of joy and happiness while creating a powerful energy for change. A powerful energy to support and create the necessary energies for change, for the shift in consciousness of humanity to move into the 5th dimensional way of life, creating Nova Earth, and peace on earth for all.

Goldie crystal skull brings a sparkle to the energetic intention and yet a scientific mind, and is a conductor of energy so magnifies all the energetic intentions of the group. The copper elements induce energy of a frequency to shift and generate a fusion of power and intention to magnify and radiate the essence of the combined energies.

George crystal skull brings the calculating energy of the scientist, the calculation and wherewithal to be the alchemist to create change to assist in the letting go of stagnant energies, and to create the opportunity for new energies, new possibilities, new potentialities, to create the environment of alchemy needed to raise the consciousness of all.

Divine timing and synchronicity

And so collectively the skull team are able to work together in myriad ways to bring about the necessary conditions to raise awareness, awaken souls, and create an environment for the possibility of peace on earth, loving kindness, living in harmony with Mother Earth, and all living beings.

The knowledge and wisdom stored in the crystals from their formation enables the connection with Mother Earth to be present at all times, and working together in Divine timing and synchronicity creates the best possible outcome for all.

This beautiful coming together of all aspects in meditation creates waves of multidimensional energy around the world bringing balance, love, peace and joy to the hearts and minds of all souls and links to their crystalline essence, the crystalline grid and Mother Earth in a truly magnificent way beloveds, and we hope you can sense the power and magnitude of all this as part of the magnificence of All That Is. Amen.

Universal Intention for the Highest and Greatest Good of All

Dear beloveds it is our joy to share more with you about the progress being made and the raising of the consciousness for all.

In your reality more souls are awakening to the fact that you are able to manifest good solutions, outcomes, situations, and opportunities for yourselves, and those which are for the highest and greatest good of all.

The understanding of quantum physics is helping to factualise a process which many thought far-fetched, and other-worldly, but a definition and confirmation from a scientific point of view has underpinned this possibility.

As souls open to their true greatness and capabilities they begin to see that a clear desire for a goal for good can be achieved through this means and this inspires and encourages them to continue to work in this way, and enjoy the benefits to be achieved.

Believing that all is energy, and that positive thoughts create a positive energy drives the understanding and intention for the brain to follow this guidance, and small initial success leads to greater opportunities.

universal intention

The intention of this 'or something better' allows the universal intention to create an outcome that is currently beyond your imaginings and one which is more suited, and beneficial, when working for your highest and greatest good. And this opportunity can be used for working for the highest and greatest good for others, and events around the world, as the principle is the same.

A statement of intent of 'this or something better' allows the creation of solutions to global issues when sufficient energy is brought to bear, hence group meditations are always more powerful than an individual one.

And so when you feel powerless through seeing all the negative news, the catastrophes around the world, you can quickly counteract this with positive energy for good and create a statement to counteract those thoughts and impressions. Feel what resonates for you, you are powerful beyond measure, stand in that power and say I AM powerful, I AM one with All That Is, I AM able to create positive change, I see the world at peace, I see all humanity living in harmony with Mother Earth, and all living beings, I see a world of love and compassion.

send unconditional love

And then use these statements, send unconditional love and white light to all situations not of the highest and greatest good, not in balance with All That Is, and ask that all souls work together for the highest and greatest good of all. 'I send unconditional love and white light and see that all decisions made to bring balance to All That Is are made for the highest and greatest good of all.'

There are many images that can be used, and in your intention and power to co-create Nova Earth, you are able to send out strong positive energies to manifest positive solutions.

At the same time you will be raising your own crystalline essence, becoming more in alignment with the Oneness of All That Is, and radiating your light for the benefit of all.

This light and love will raise the energies of the crystalline grid and support the awakening of all souls on this journey.

We love you and bless you, honour you and thank you for all your endeavours toward co-creating Nova Earth, the new Golden Age for all. Amen.

Free Will and Choice

Beloveds, we continue to share insights and offer wisdoms accumulated over eons of time for humanity to consider on their journey, for all is free will and choice, and no two souls will resonate exactly with the insights in the same way so please take that which resonates with you and set aside that which does not.

For the beauty of free will and choice is that it allows you to fully experience that which you came here to do, and there is so much information available and information to be released, that you could not possibly absorb all this.

Free will and choice allows you to follow your soul's desire at that time knowing that it can and will change and alter as your consciousness expands, and this can be done without guilt or fear that you are on the wrong path or 'should' be following some train of thought or information released through various means.

It is in your own and humanity's interest to follow that which interests you, that which you are passionate about because you are an energetic match with it, it is what you came here to experience and discover, you will benefit from following your dream rather than following that which you feel you ought to follow.

This allows for discernment in the information you follow, it allows you to be selective and that is not saying that other information is incorrect or irrelevant, it is just that it is not of your interest at this moment and may or may not become of your interest at a later stage.

Following your dream becomes easier in the new energies as patterns of expected behaviour dissolve and old ways of being adapt to the new, light energies where more opportunities exist, and manifestation of your dreams becomes easier.

In this way as each soul follows their true path and purpose, the solutions to the issues currently being faced by humanity will arise and manifest to support the ascension and awakening of all souls and Mother Earth. For we are looking at heart-centred thoughts and actions, heart-centred inspirations that work for the highest and greatest good of all, for when you are connected to your God-self, your love essence, how can this not be true? When love is the energy of the time, and you radiate that love, then your inspirations will be based on creating inner peace for yourself and all others; for creating a loving environment for yourself and all others, and so information and solutions flourish from this pure essence within enlightened souls.

Solutions to many issues are already being discovered as newer souls recognise a need for action, and from their passion create a solution to resolve this issue, and raise awareness and create a better, brighter future which in turn inspires others to follow their passion too. As souls see that these manifestations are possible, then the energy focuses to continue this path to work for the highest and greatest good of all.

Your world is changing. Light workers have held the energy of the Blueprint for earth, the energy for the Divine Plan for all, and in this new energy much of this is manifesting now. Ways and means are evolving to improve life for more souls not just the few. Awareness for the need for equality, justice, harmony between all living beings; peace, acceptance, gratitude, fairness, respect for all living beings, and the oneness with All That Is throughout this planet, solar system, universe, omniverse, and beyond.

We see the light radiating stronger and stronger each day as humanity collectively awakens to their ability to create change, to be the change, to believe in the possibility of a new way of living, and co-create the new Golden Age, Nova Earth, a 5th dimensional way of life for all.

So beloveds, follow your dream, follow your passion, and know that from a heart-centred position you will be fulfilling your true path and purpose, and supporting the creation of peace for all, and a new way of life for this and future generations, and we honour and thank you from our hearts for this benevolence. Amen, beloveds and so it is.

The Gift of Crystal Skulls

Beloveds, we have talked about the crystal skulls and how much a part they are in the overall Divine Plan. We know, and understand, the power and capabilities of crystals, and when carved into this shape they become even more focussed, concentrated and powerful in these energies.

Additionally they are formed in this way, a way that humans can logically accept them as a friend and that the 'brain' aspect of the head may impart information and wisdom, and in this way energetic connections are formed, and information downloaded.

The Mitchell-Hedges skull, one of the most well-known skulls, still holds the mystery of how it was formed, as man in the 3rd dimension, can only compare its formation to the machinery and equipment which is currently available. But as is gently being released, and made known as information, there are many technologies and capabilities that are not currently in man's awareness but have been used before.

sources of power

Humanity is currently awakening to the fact that previous civilizations were advanced in different facets of technology. See the interest in the pyramids, how were they built, why were they built, how were they in alignment with certain stars, and placed where they are?

Why are pyramids in Egypt, why have crystals been found near sites of pyramids, and so on?

These questions and discoveries will continue, as the pieces are unravelled and revealed, when humanity is ready to accept the information.

How did the Mayans know and plan their Calendars, how did they prepare their prophesies? How did the Atlanteans have such sophisticated technology, and sources of power beyond current understanding?

All these mysteries and information are gently being unfolded, and as pieces revealed and the overall pictures established, a greater understanding will emerge, and an acceptance of the capabilities of civilisations previously in existence will occur.

And the existence of crystal skulls like the Mitchell-Hedges provide a source of mystery, enigma, beauty, and a desire to uncover the truth, to understand its origin, and what it can show us and help us understand, and so its discovery plays an important role in the understanding of things beyond our current experience.

gifts to humanity

And in the same way, the discovery of the other crystal skulls, and those ancient ones who show how they were made still hold mysteries. Why were they made, who made them, what can they demonstrate to us today?

These skulls are such gifts beloveds, they are gifted to humanity to bring awareness, to bring love, to bring wonder and awe, and to share wisdoms. They also work together to help bring healing to the world, and work with their guardians to link heaven and earth, to bring joy and happiness, and lessen the veil which exists between our higher selves, and our earthly bodies.

They connect us to our crystalline essence in a very powerful way, they raise the energies of the crystalline grid, they light up the world with their individual personalities and characteristics, they link generations and civilisations through their existence, they hold information ready to be released at the appropriate time, they are connected to the crystals in the centre of the earth, and those within and without the earth, and so are regularly adjusting to the vibrational frequency.

Bless the skulls, beloveds, and if you have one, honour its gifts, work with it to bring love into the world, to bring lightness, compassion, joy and healing, and all will be well, beloveds, all will be well.

We honour you; we salute you and thank you for all your endeavours in creating Nova Earth, the new Golden Age, and for holding the love and light of God in your hearts and minds. Amen.

Bringing the Completion of Love to this Planet

We share our loving thoughts with all souls who resonate on this level of crystal energies, for all souls are linked through the crystal highway, although for some the connection is stronger than for others. Likewise some souls consciously wish to expand, and raise this connection, as part of their soul growth and some remain unawakened to their connection. For some others they are aware of their connection although their role in this lifetime directs their energies and intentions in other directions.

And so we see a melting pot of intentions and attention to this phenomenon for all souls on earth. The beauty of this option is that all souls on earth have free will and choice, and so may therefore choose to awaken or not, to focus on growth and expansion or not, and within the choice of growth and expansion there are many, many ways to explore this.

And free will and choice makes available the opportunity to refocus on another area of growth, or diverse ways to fulfil the soul mission, and fulfil the purpose for choosing to be here on earth at this time.

For this auspicious time on earth allows for many diverse opportunities to fulfil collective roles, and individual soul growth, although as all souls are part of the oneness of the soul collective, you each benefit from all other energies from other soul's life experiences.

experience life on earth

So there is no right or wrong, there is no judgement, it just is, and all energies make the whole, and this is the wholeness of experience of life on earth.

Over millennia souls have experienced light and dark, they have experienced compassion and love, and also lack of love and compassion, and it is now at this time that the light is bringing the completion of love to this planet. And this has been ordained, at this time, in conjunction with Mother Earth as humanity has passed the marker time in 2012 for this to occur.

In previous civilisations the light did not become the will of the people, it did not become the oneness and wholeness of all souls, and so these civilisations ceased to exist despite many learning's, and aspects of love and light within them.

In this civilisation, the light has reached a point of growth and expansion, and the will of the people has reached a level to sustain life on earth, to correct the imbalances, to regain the higher energies, and to co-create Nova Earth, the new Golden Age for all souls.

for those who desire peace

Those who do not wish to participate through a decision made before this lifetime, or who have remained asleep to the opportunities in this lifetime, may choose to move to a different space where they may continue in this way. For those who desire peace, who desire to live in harmony with All That Is, who desire to see Mother Earth healthy, happy and fulfilling her soul purpose, the energies will continue to raise to bring fulfilment of this desire.

And this will take time, as many energies are deeply entrenched, as those who have most to lose from the old energies are least willing to forgo their ill-gotten gains, and to move into a time of equality, fairness and love. Those who have lived by controlling life on earth, who have hidden agendas, and who are reluctant to adapt to the New Earth will find it harder to let go of long held power. But this is a false power, a false existence, and not of the light, and will not hold up in the new energies; it cannot be, it cannot exist going forward into the New Earth.

And new technologies are being given to support all humanity and remove the control from larger corporations.

The DNA of new souls emerging will not accommodate the old ways, and will work to adapt and change ways of existence.

creating new ways

The new human beings born will already be part of the New Earth energies, and will not work with the existing ways, they will create new ways, they will form new concepts, new ideas, new ways of being that will move forwards in love and light that will sweep the old ways aside.

The new energies will bring in ways and means of living that offer love, equality, fairness, peace, joy, happiness, and so on, that will create the new opportunities for all.

And so beloveds, dream, meditate and be open to the new ways of being, to change and adaptation, to being part of this new experience that was prophesied for all in the Divine Plan, the Blueprint for all, and celebrate being here at this time, co-creating this amazing life for all, and Mother Earth, and all living beings.

We love you and thank you all beloveds, thank you.

Recalibration of Mother Earth

Crystals are a source of light, and of healing, and are multifunctional with many purposes. They are also beings of light with their own journey, and purpose, as all beings of light and all souls are in this lifetime.

All aspects of life from the smallest animal to the largest tree, to crystals, humans, weather elements, all are aspects of the oneness that make up the whole, and make your experience of life on earth.

For you are a being of light beloveds, you are a part of the original light sent out to experience duality, separation and non-light, you are all aspects of the oneness of All That Is created to experience different aspects of life on earth.

And in the Blueprint for life on earth, now is the time of the Great Turning, of the changes being bought about to bring into alignment, non-duality, non-separation and non-darkenss, and bring all into alignment in the light and love of God, Source, the Great Provider who created all of this.

Your physical being enables you to live on planet earth, to experience the energies of separation and duality, of non-love, and non-light, and this can manifest as pain and illness as a means of exhibiting the non-alignment with oneness. This was a given way of indicating that non-alignment exists, and a way for you to look at your lifestyle, and choose how to make changes in your thoughts and perceptions to bring you back into alignment.

And no, beloveds this is not said as a judgement, criticism, or fault finding; this is not a statement that you have created illness in yourself, nor are you guilty of any wrong doing. It was given as an indication that life on earth is out of balance, that pollution creates ill health, that excessive stress and working hours/conditions creates illness, that the imbalance of those who have little on this earth compared to those who have too much, that time denied spending time relaxing in nature, with family and friends through the hustle and bustle of life, cause this non-alignment.

That the food produced and eaten is not the most healthy and energetically well balanced, it could be, and the news and information fed to the population is not always in alignment with the truth.

The way that corporations are based on returning a profit, and not on the well-being of all, and Mother Earth, contributes to the misalignment, and so we could go on.

The Great Turning

At this time of the Great Turning, or the Event, as it is also called, life on earth is changing. Souls are awakening to this misalignment; souls are looking to repair the damage to the oceans and rivers, to bring back balance and harmony to the waters, and make them clear, clean, and healthy again.

Focus is being given to those in need in many directions, to bring about balance, equality, fairness, justice, and harmony. Focus is given to healthy food, time in nature, meditations, natural healing methods and products. Focus is on justice for all souls, and peace on earth for all people.

As this energy and intention grow, so Mother Earth heals and restores, so all living beings feel the energetic changes, and recalibration takes place.

As light workers continue to hold and raise the energy of the crystalline grid, the crystals within and without the earth also raise their energies, and these are then reflected back to humanity, and Mother Earth. As this occurs, so the hearts and minds of all souls awaken, and adapt to the new energies.

new waves of love light

Support from all beings within your orbit is being lovingly given, and new waves of love light are being granted to further support this process, and given the passing of the marker a point of no return in the process of realignment, all energies and intentions are focussed on bringing this about in Divine timing.

So beloveds, we thank all souls who are actively contributing to this realignment, through agriculture, technology, science, environment, peace, global meditations, information sharing, light holding, awareness, justice, equality, empowerment, and many, many other means that are adding to the return of balance and harmony with all things. To the realignment of humanity, Mother Earth, all living beings in the oneness of All That Is, and the connection between all things.

And crystals continue their role as they have done since the beginning of your concept of time, to hold and maintain the balance of energies, and to release the wisdoms appropriate to the time.

They hold the remembrance in the Akashic records, they hold the Blueprint for earth. They bring love, healing, comfort, joy, enlightenment, balance, beauty, and a connection to the Source of all things.

Enjoy all the gifts given to you, and see all things as part of the whole, and as part of the plan for reconnection, and realignment to the energies of love, compassion, peace, and harmony, world without end. Amen.

Imagine life on Nova Earth – this can be yours

As the collective consciousness grows and expands, the light quotient from this also expands and adds light and love to the crystalline grid, to the crystalline essence of your physicality, to the crystals in the centre of the earth, the earth's crust, and without the earth. This ever expanding light love energy is inhaled, and ingested, physically by all living beings, by Mother Earth, and by all humanity, by all natural elements, trees, plants, soil, sand, and grasslands, and by water in all its forms.

The air becomes lighter and brighter, and the circular effect of this increases the continuous flow of light.

Added to this the solar flares, the influx of light energies, and the loving support from all forms; angels, unicorns, elementals, dragons, and so on, reflects the love available to all humanity to assist in the process of ascension, and co-creating Nova Earth.

And as you can understand this process takes time, and cannot be achieved without due process. The effect of too much light love energy on a physical being would be unbearable, and would not allow time for the integration, and understanding of each new process. In the same way a person beginning lessons in any sport could not suddenly become at the top of their game as it were, without learning each stage, gaining in fitness and experience, and gradually making their way to a more proficient level with the sport.

Thus humanity must needs take the time to adjust to each new wave of light influx, and to each newly expanded awareness of the universe, to gain confidence in each understanding and implement any changes.

It also demonstrates that the rate of change for humans individually is different depending on many things; where they are in their life experience and current circumstances, their willingness and ability to make changes, their chosen life purpose, and all previous life experiences, their openness to the possibility of a blueprint for earth, and the co-creation of a different way of life for all.

And there is no right or wrong in any of this, in the same way that the crystals change and adapt to the conditions on earth, and the collective consciousness. And this is all done in accordance with the Divine Plan laid down for all humanity, and Mother Earth, working in oneness to create a life of peace, abundance, joy, happiness, creativity, fulfilment and harmony for all.

gaining insights

As new technologies become available, as new awareness grows of the challenges to be overcome, of the need for all basic human needs to be fulfilled, to restore balance and harmony with Mother Earth, then consciousness grows and spreads to all souls, and those who came to earth to see the fulfilment of this plan are diligently working to see it come to fruition, and are receiving support, love, and insights from many different sources.

To gain more insights and to connect more deeply with the collective consciousness, with the support being made available to you, and to the crystalline grid, link and connect to your crystals and crystal skulls to gain insights, revelations, love and a stronger connection to Mother Earth through their resonance. Connect to your crystal skulls for deeper connections to All That Is, and the collective crystal skull consciousness, and enjoy the myriad connections, and strengthen your intuition.

this can be your life

So many amazing events are unfolding; so many significant events are occurring in the earth plane that we watch with great joy and excitement for the co-creation of Nova Earth, and a new way of life for all, and this will be glorious beyond words, and beyond your imaginations.

Imagine a news programme on your TV with no war reports, no announcements of the numbers killed, no mothers losing their children through war, no houses bombed and people made homeless, no people left abandoned, and hungry through war, no townships and communities destroyed, and no animals hurt or killed in the process.

Imagine a news programme with no reports of refugee camps, no pictures of hungry, starving children with a lack of medicine and hygienic conditions, no distraught parents struggling to cope.

Instead see a news programme of happy events, people coming together for concerts, music, poetry, creativity, in harmony, peace, safety and happiness.

See beaches and water, clean, free from pollution, free from damage, and see people swimming, enjoying family days on the beach, looking at the healthy sea-life and pond life, see the dolphins and whales out at sea connecting with humanity, safely, respectfully, joyfully, sharing information in subtle energetic exchanges.

See healthy food reports, and know that all foods are grown in rich soil, providing nutritious food, in plentiful supply for all people on earth; healthy children all over the world eating wholesome plentiful food.

Imagine these scenarios, imagine these good news stories of equality, respect, happiness, community support, and joy, and this can be your life on earth beloveds, it can be yours.

We leave you with these images to enjoy, and to add to the collective consciousness energies for all.

You Have Been a Co-creator for Eons of Time

Beloveds it is our desire to share today how the energetic imprint for the new Golden Age has been building momentum, and how this will manifest in divine timing and perfection.

In a simple way it is about love, about love of self, of others, of all living beings, and planet earth, for love is the energy of divinity, and all is love.

Over the years as souls have awakened to this wisdom which has always been there, and is always held within the crystals within and without the earth, then the love heart resonance has grown, and this helps souls shed that which was not of their true nature. The duality and separation aspects of the soul which were adopted in order to experience non-love and non-balance exhibited in hate, segregation, conflict, greed, and many other traits not in alignment with oneness, and divine love.

As more hearts open to the love available to them, then they see the misalignment, and return to the wisdoms of the ancients, and move back into oneness, and back into alignment with divine love, and this brings changes in their inner world which reflect in the outer world.

And this is evidenced in your world with many changes occurring creating a great sense of community, of reappraisal of priorities, of coming together in like-minded groups to rebalance, and restore harmony in your world. It also exhibits in the awareness of the need to address the damage caused by pollution, by waste products, by conflicts, by materialism, and by separation.

And now groups are dedicating themselves to clearing the damage from the oceans, the waters, the land and air – all the elements of life on earth. In this way it assists Mother Earth in rebalancing, and restoring harmony to her being which in turn rebalances weather patterns, and assists all life forms.

So love as the essence of all things is at the heart of co-creating the new Golden Age.

And alongside this is the will, and determination, of souls who have been working tirelessly, for many lifetimes even, to sow the seeds for this transformation. Recall how many souls have over their lifetime dedicated themselves to peace, to technology to assist the earth, to humanitarian causes, to awareness of pollution. And many times, whilst remembered, they have been side-lined as odd, as unrealistic, or even just ignored because other souls were not ready to listen, or did not feel they had the power to do anything, or did not feel in alignment with the information and message.

And yet these souls bravely sowed the seeds of awareness, of wisdoms, of information that have grown over time, and in these times, more souls are adding to this wisdom, and taking practical action to address these issues.

And yes there are still many un-awakened souls who say, oh nothing can be done, it's too late, I can't do anything, but these souls are becoming less and less.

sensing the change

In addition they are beginning to see the changes being made, to see the power of people making changes, the power of people to demonstrate their desire for change; for there to be no conflict, for there to be an end to poverty and inequality, for an end to injustice and control by the few over the many.

Souls are stepping into their power, and the next generation of souls are taking up the pace, and continuing with this energy. They have come into this life in a different energy; they are sensing the change, and have come with a different purpose. The momentum to create a better, brighter, fairer world is in their DNA, it is in their beingness, and they are bringing new technology, new innovations and new energies. They are reigniting the connections to star seeds, to the ancient wisdoms, and are bringing through the energies of peace, equality, fairness and justice, joy, freedom, and harmony, and this will continue with each generation onwards.

So continue to dream of how you would like to see the future, continue to send out energies of love, of gratitude, of peace, love yourselves and others, acknowledge your self-worth and that of others, and know you truly are magnificent, and truly are capable of standing in your power and co-creating the new earth, a life of peace for all.

And know also that you have been part of this process through many lifetimes, setting out the energetic imprint for it to be held for this time, for the creation of Nova Earth, the ascension of earth, and for a joyful, creative, harmonious existence on this planet.

You have been a co-creator for eons of time beloveds, and this is now the time for manifestation of the collective consciousness held within the crystals within and without Mother Earth for all souls, all living beings, and Mother Earth, and the manifestation of life in oneness with All That Is.

We thank you, and love you, and honour you beloveds. Amen till time again.

Setting the Energetic Intention

Beloveds we explained about setting the intention for Nova Earth, many eons of time ago, and now is the time for the manifestation of this way of life.

When using the word time, it is difficult to explain in our terms, as your time, your man-made time is not our concept, and so it is often misunderstood. Time is an energy, a universal energy, and therefore not linear, and not specific.

In your time you are able to say, I will meet you at 10am tomorrow because your time can be that specific on the basis of how your minds work, and the way of life on earth. At times, you change the time to suit the seasons, proving that time is a moveable feast as it were, and therefore not a given or a constant.

Different countries around the world are in different time zones, again proving that life can, and does, exist when not all working to the same time. When you travel to another country you are able to adapt your time to that country, and change it back again afterwards. Beloveds, time even in your defined world is flexible and moveable, and yet your system still functions.

universal energy

Our reference to time or 'a time' is the way we can communicate with you, and refer not to a specific time, but a time when the universal energies are in alignment for events to occur or energies to change, therefore we could substitute the words universal energy for time, and this might help you to see this concept.

The Blueprint for Nova Earth was cast eons of time ago, and all put in place through all manner of ways to assist the unfoldment of God's will, and the new Golden Age on earth. And this has occurred on other planets over eons of time in a myriad of ways.

Life on earth gives free will and choice, and this has led to previous civilizations making decisions not in alignment with the energies of the Divine Plan, and therefore they ceased to move into the new level of energetic existence.

Your civilization beloveds, has passed this marker, and therefore the energies of earth have reached a level enabling the next stage of unfoldment to occur.

To support this unfoldment many events, and continued endeavours from around the universe and beyond, are continually offering information, updates, insights, love, answering questions, and so on. Influxes of light are sent to earth, and the light is outshining the old paradigm, and creating signs of a new way of life emerging.

creating Nova Earth

Light Workers, love holders, way showers, new innovations, technologies, environmental endeavours, sustainability in agriculture and lifestyle, reducing pollution, and so on are all contributing to changing the energies on earth to be in alignment with the energies of the Blueprint, the universal energies for creating Nova Earth. And this is a gradual process of life on earth, and all those involved and awakened souls continue to raise awareness and energies for all souls on earth.

As more souls awaken, and step aside from the fear based 3D outlook, as more souls awaken to their individual and collective power and potential to make changes, and bring more love and compassion into the world, then the overall collective consciousness raises.

As this collective consciousness matches the universal energies of the Blueprint for the new Golden Age, the two merge, and life on earth changes, so we cannot talk about a time for this to happen. We are in this time of happening, the 'event' is happening although it is not related to a time in general or a specific time, just a matching and blending of energies.

So your saying of 'when the time is right' or in 'Divine timing' literally means when the energies match, and the outcome will be for the highest and greatest good of all as decreed in the Blueprint for earth.

And this event will continue to grow, and expand, as humanity becomes more and more loving, and compassionate, and more and more changes occur to bring equality, fairness, justice, peace, harmony, and joy.

Knowledge, insights, and information will continue to be revealed, and thus the process of awakening is ongoing, and your lives will continue to grow and expand.

dream big

So dream big, expand your thoughts of how you would like life to be, connect to your ancient wisdoms, and bring those in alignment with the now. Celebrate the evolution of humanity, of Mother Earth, and all living beings; celebrate the positive changes in your life, and that of others.

The eternal peace for mankind, the beauty of Mother Earth, the equality of all souls, the joy of the sunset and sunrise, your health and well-being, the greater awareness of the gifts given to you in all ways; the healing of the souls of all mankind, Mother Earth, and all living beings to have this physical experience of life on earth. Your dreams will assist in manifesting this life by adding to the collective energies, by upgrading the crystalline grid, the crystals within the earth, and your own crystalline essence.

How magnificent is all this beloveds, how truly magnificent an experience as part of your total soul growth, and expansion? World without end, Amen.

Celebrate All That You Are

Beloveds we are delighted to add to the text and energy of this book. At the time of writing, or channelling and transcribing, we are in the same time/moment that you are now reading these words.

And part of the purpose for creating this book at the time of preparation was to set an energetic intention in preparation for you reading these words at the right time for you. All souls will be drawn to read these words, and feel these energies when it is right for them, and that will vary significantly.

In the meantime as the book is being created, the energetic imprint of our insights and visions is being created ahead of that time if you will.

The significance of creating these words is to lay down the imprint, and for it to be manifest in a written, visible form which is then added to the previous text of the book thus far created. As each new insight is transmitted it enhances the imprint already in existence in its file on the computer. So the seeds are already being sown, and once added to the text of the book, the energies are emitted through the crystal highway on the computer, out and around, to be added to the energies of the crystalline grid, the crystals within and without the earth, and to the crystalline essence for all souls.

appearing in the Now

So although these words are not published at the time of writing they are sending out energies, and adding to the overall energetic imprint already in existence. This imprint gets upgraded with each new influx of light granted to earth, the raising of the collective consciousness, and the opening of the heart centres of awakened souls.

By the time you read the words, or by the time the work is published, the finished article is in alignment with the energies prevalent at the time of reading, as to appear in the Now, and of the moment.

It is sometimes challenging for our partner to continue being devoted to creating these books which actually appear to have little impact, and do not appear on the Top Best Sellers list, but we reassure our beloved, and those souls who read these words, that from the original intention of transcribing these words to the completion of the work, every thought, every moment spent channelling, writing, typing, checking and thinking of the book adds exponentially to its impact, and we encourage our beloved Lindsay to recognise her endeavours, commitment and dedication to completing this, the third in The Way Forward series, and reassure all that the overall impact of all 3 books has contributed hugely to raising the energies, as has that of all souls who channel, and share their abilities, and we thank them, and those of you who are reading these words for your contribution to creating Nova Earth.

Each physical book acts as a transmitter, and so wherever around the world that physical book happens to be, it is working to raise the energies for all souls.

the new Golden Age

The content of the book; the information, the revelations, the vision for the future all help to inform, upgrade, update, and create interest in the world around you and beyond, as your consciousness expands on the bigger picture.

Setting down the vision for Nova Earth helps to create this template, and so we encourage you to dream big in your imaginings of the new Golden Age.

Sense and feel the peace around you sense and feel the unconditional love for all living beings, and Mother Earth. Sense and feel the joy and harmony of existence on planet earth. Look up and out to the stars as part of the oneness of All That Is, and sense the unity of all the universe.

Marvel at the new technology creating sustainable, clean energy. Marvel at the community spirit of groups working together in oneness for the highest and greatest good of all.

Delight in the creative opportunities for entertainment, poetry, art, and theatre. Be amazed at the opportunities to travel quickly, safely and free from pollution around the world to see spectacular sights, and meet with friends and family.

Sense the vitality and health in food grown organically, lovingly, sustainably, and the nourishment to your cells and benefits to your well-being. See children developing their skills and talents safely, supportively, and lovingly.

See beauty in nature and Mother Earth, and enjoy the awesome sights, and sounds of being outdoors.

All this, and more, will create your reality, create the world you wish to live in, and raise your families in. See the light glowing, and celebrate your role in co-creating this glorious existence.

I AM a Master of Light.
I AM love.
I AM a wondrous co-creator of Nova Earth.
I AM one with all things.
I AM at one with the universe.
I AM at one with Mother Earth, and all living beings.
I AM peace, I radiate loving peace for all.
I AM whole and complete as I AM in the eyes of God.

I AM a divine being in the here and now radiating light and love.
I AM harmonious with all things.
I shine my light in loving gratitude for all life, and the gifts and bounty of Mother Earth.
Amen.

Celebrate, dream, meditate, and honour all that you are, and your co-creation of Nova Earth, for it shall be yours beloveds, it shall be yours. Amen.

When the I AM becomes WE ARE ONE

Beloveds, we delight in further communications with you through this method which is just one of the ways that energies are shared. For some people listening is the greatest way of absorbing energies, for others it is visual and others reading. Whichever way or combination you prefer, you are still absorbing energies through all means as each thought, spoken word, and visual output, all emit energies which are available for those who wish to avail themselves of them on all levels.

And this is a matter of free choice for those, who on a higher level, have agreed to be open to the higher energies through all means.

The information, intention, love and light from all means of sharing, are adding to the collective energies to raise the vibrations for all; for Mother Earth, for all living beings, the crystalline grid, and thereby the crystalline essence within your body. All this is turn helps to awaken further DNA within the body to be more receptive to the higher energies, and release more capabilities within the human body so that you may further experience a greater vision of the bigger picture.

How amazing is it that all this occurs just through seeing, reading or hearing messages of love and good intent shared with like-minded souls in joint co-creation of Nova Earth?

inner knowing

And further supporting this are the crystals given and created by your Creator through Mother Earth which hold the love and light, the Blueprint for earth, and the wisdom and knowledge to accomplish this. As the connection between your crystalline essence, the crystalline grid, and the crystals within and without the earth grows in strength and vibration, so on an energetic level your connection with the oneness of all things grows and your connection with All That Is grows, and your I AM becomes WE ARE ONE in oneness, and the energetic level of the collective consciousness grows and expands exponentially.

So the energies for co-creating Nova Earth become more potent, and your connection to your inner knowing, and remembrance of all things, becomes greater.

Enjoy sitting quietly and connecting to your inner knowing and remembrance of all things, consciously connect to the crystalline grid, to the crystals within and without the earth, connect to your personal crystals, and crystal skulls or photos of crystals, and enjoy the resonance of all the love and light, the wisdom of the ages, and the Divine Plan to create Nova Earth.

See the world through the eyes of love, and see life in Nova Earth how you wish it to be. See love in the hearts of all souls, see joy in the eyes of all children; see the energy radiating from trees and plants, and the enhanced beauty in nature. Appreciate the gifts of life, wholesome food, the company of friends, the fun in creativity, the sharing of stories, the lightness of life in all ways; the healthy lifestyle, the warmth of the sun, the wisdom of the ancients, the balance and harmony of all things, and the joy of life for all beings on earth at this auspicious time.

We are with you beloveds, supporting your endeavours, and guiding, and assisting humanity to co-create the new Golden Age as prophesised for all. We send our greatest love as always, amen beloveds.

Unity Consciousness for the New Golden Age

Beloveds, we begin to draw to a close the insights shared with you through this method. We thank our devoted Lindsay for her determination and diligence in following her inner guidance to complete this third book in The Way Forward series, and look forward to more titles in the future if she is willing to continue in this way.

We are drawing to a close as we have set the intention for creating Nova Earth and this is the energy of the title 'The Way Forward' series; this is the culmination of the imprint that was desired by Jesus. The Way Forward is to co-create the new Golden Age and these 3 books have set, and held, the intention for this to manifest, each word, thought, action and deed involved in the creation of this series has added to the imprint to create, and hold, the energy for this to be manifest.

In creating ahead of time as you know it, the energies have continued to raise in reaching the level for manifestation which is where you will be by the time you read these words.

crystal consciousness

Crystals are like computers, they can be programmed, energised, rebooted, reprogrammed to work alongside the creation of Nova Earth. They can be used for your well-being, for communication and support in your daily life, to bring light and love into your home, to create grids for healing, and peace in situations both personal, and of the world.

They are beautiful, can be carried in your pocket, worn as jewellery, be used in your timepieces and technology, they can even make time speed up.

They can protect you, bring love into your heart-centre, assist your chakras in opening and balancing; help you sleep, relieve pain, and support you lovingly through difficult times.

Thus we connect you to the title of this book Crystal Consciousness as all things on this planet, and within this planet, are linked and connected to crystals.

Our bodies are connected to crystals, our crystal highways allow global communication on the co-creating of Nova Earth, and the spreading of love and peace.

Lemurian crystals link us to the wisdom of the ancients, and to their way of life connected and honouring Mother Earth, and all living beings.

These gifts from God are given to support the co-creation of Nova Earth, the ascension of Gaia and all humanity, and the crystal consciousness which connects us in a loving embrace creating oneness of All That Is, and the unity consciousness for the new Golden Age.

Enjoy your crystals, your collective consciousness through them, and celebrate the co-creation of Nova Earth, holding the light and love of God in your hearts for today and always. Amen beloveds Amen.

A Loving Intention for Humanity

Beloveds, this is our final message for this book, and we thank you for receiving our messages, and intentions of love, during the creation of this work. As has been explained, the loving energy created from the first moment of the thought given to our partner Lindsay for the very first book has grown, and expanded, over the time-frame of the creation of this series.

Each thought, conversation, action, transcription and so on, have created a magnificent energy of loving intention for humanity, as have all books created with this loving intention to support humanity's awakening.

All seed thoughts laid down in advance to be expanded, pondered on, talked about, and integrated into your systems, have raised the overall energies of love, and awakened consciousness as part of the collective consciousness for all humanity, all living beings, and Mother Earth.

As your awareness grows, and you begin to see the bigger picture and the potentiality for a world of peace, happiness and harmony, so you notice that there are many wonderful things already happening.

a new way of living

And as awareness of the world events which are now openly reported occurs, so you seek out the alternative news feeds, the ones which show human endeavours in sustainability, renewable energy, conservation, equality, justice, peace, community, and delight in knowing these events are occurring globally, and gaining a momentum all of their own.

And we are not suggesting this will happen overnight as there are many energies still stuck in the old ways, and many souls reluctant to change their approach. But the new souls coming in are of the new energy, and are stating their intentions, and making clear their belief in a new way of living, being and existing in the world.

So the balance begins to change, and those old souls who have for years been raising the energies, and holding the light, and making all this possible, can celebrate the emergence of new ideas and ways, and these will be integrated into mainstream media and life for all.

Be patient, meditate on how you wish the world to be, how you see the future for the next generations, how you see Mother Earth, healthy and radiating her beauty, and be grateful for being here, in a physical body at this auspicious time, for this is the experience you chose to have, and it is a magnificent time for you in your total lifetimes on earth, and your soul growth.

Relish each new change for a better way of life, a healthier life, a more harmonious life, and one where all hearts beat as one, and all hearts are open and awakened fully to the love that is available to them, and the beauty of life on earth.

Thank you beloveds and we look forward to communicating with you in further ways in your future times.

Go well beloveds till time again with our greatest love. Amen.

Extras

Elestial Crystal - I am a Power House of Love

I am the generator crystal; I am a power house of love. I share and radiate this love with all humanity, all living beings, and Mother Earth from whence I came.

I have stored inside my beingness the history of the earth, its movements, changes, aspirations, her need to clear and cleanse, to move forwards towards her own ascension.

You must needs understand that the creation of Mother Earth came with her own ascension plan, her own role within the Divine Plan, as well as providing a home for humanity, and all living beings. As well as providing water, shelter, food, a climatic system, and existence within the planetary system of this solar system as part of the totality of the universe. And this plan for her own growth has been going on since her conception, the movement of the plates within her being, the volcanoes, earthquakes, climate changes, all these and more, are part of her total growth and evolution, and this will continue to change and adapt for eons of time to come.

We are in existence, at this time, as part of the plan for this time, but the Divine Plan has been in existence since the creation of the earth, and so has been going on long before humanity arrived on earth, and will continue to evolve as part of the universe and beyond. The mind of man is limited in understanding to what he is experiencing, is open to receive, and what information is made available to him. The life and existence of the planet and solar system is far greater, and therefore man cannot totally comprehend the total picture, although he is often tempted to believe he can.

And so as Mother Earth continues on her journey, and must needs cleanse herself of all miscreations, let alone clear those that mankind has inflicted on her, then events continue to unfold. Many are unseen and take centuries to complete, but some as in the dramatic weather conditions of 2017, are more evident.

And even so despite the outward appearance of chaos and disaster to life and property these events are assisting Mother Earth, and assisting humanity to go back to their roots, to help and support each other to work together, to find hope and love among their fellow man, and do without the way of life that had become prevalent; the money, the material goods, the suspicion of each other, the separation created by media, and others. People are rediscovering their oneness, discovering the things that unite them not separate them, and becoming heart-centred in unity not separated by imagined concepts.

And so whilst we send love and support to all those in need and suffering, we see a positive outcome of oneness; clearing, cleansing, reprioritising, awakening of consciousness as part of the overall movement necessary to change life on earth, and moving towards Nova Earth, a time for humanity to rebalance, to unite in harmony, respect for Mother Earth, and all living beings.

I am the generator crystal sending love, heartfulness, hope, strength, courage, optimism, awakening and support for the changes needed to create Nova Earth for all to live in peace and harmony once and for all, world without end. Amen.

We are Love, We are One

We are love, we are one,
We are one with all living beings
We are one with the love of God
We are love.

We are love, we are one
We are one with Mother Earth
We are one with the love of God
We are love.

We are love, we are one
We are one with the moon and stars
We are one with the love of God
We are love.

We are love, we are one
We are one with the crystal energies of light
We are one with the love of God
We are love.

We are love, we are one
We are one with the trees and the birds
We are one with the love of God
We are love.

We are love, we are one
We are one with the mountains and the plains
We are one with the love of God
We are love.

We are love, we are one
We are one with all humanity
We are one with the love of God
We are love.

We are love, we are one
We are one with the universe and beyond
We are one with the love of God
We are love.

We are love, we are one

We are one with the omniverse and beyond
We are one with the love of God
We are love.

We are love, we are one.
We are one with the love of God
We are one, we are love.

We are one with you beloveds

We are one with you beloveds, as you are one with us.

We co-exist in this lifetime as we have over many lifetimes on this planet earth.

We are all multidimensional; we are all time lords, space dust, multifaceted beings in different energy forms in this creation.

We hold the wisdom and knowledge, and the imprint of the Divine Plan for earth, as your Akashic record holds the imprint of all your lifetimes on earth.

We are the gate-keepers, the record holders, the constant beings of light in this time-frame.

We are all connected through our crystalline grid, our crystalline essence, our crystal beings within and without the earth, seen and unseen, known and unknown, and understood and not understood.

We are one in constant change, and ever increasing radiant beings of light, as created by Source for this lifetime experience on planet earth, world without end.

We radiate our light to attract the attention of awakening humanity, and work with you through many means, and assist you in many ways, and this is our joy to connect with you at this auspicious time.

We honour, love, thank and appreciate our connection with you to work together to bring in and establish the Divine Plan for earth, in love, compassion, acceptance, understanding, harmony and joy, and so it is beloveds. And so it is, Amen.

The New Earth Begins!

See the light beloveds, see it shining bright.

See it in the hearts and minds of all souls.

See it in the radiance of plants, trees, and all nature.

Hear it in the birdsong.

See the waters clear and clean, and flowing with ease and grace.

See the skies pure blue, and radiant with light.

See the compassion and love in the eyes of humanity, the understanding and accepting of differences.

See the willingness to work together in harmony looking after the forests, beaches, and plains.

See all souls working together making decisions for the highest and greatest good of all.

See gatherings of souls celebrating peace.

See all people homed in appropriate ways to meet their needs, and all souls fed with healthy food.

See children playing safely in their community, and hear their joy and laughter.

See the elderly respected and cared for, and honoured for their wisdom and knowledge.

See all animals respected and living in healthy, safe environments with respectful relationships with humanity.

See the stars shining brighter in the sky, and the sun bringing warmth and light.

See the trees standing tall in their beauty clearing the air in their special way.

Sense the feeling of love among all peoples when wars are a distant memory, and peace abounds.

Sense the feeling of well-being as souls are free from illnesses which no longer exist, and where people have access to natural healing ways as a regular occurrence.

See ways of fast travel allowing you to explore the world without pollution.

Sense the relaxed atmosphere as souls no longer have long commutes to work, and stressful jobs.

Take in the difference which will be the way of things in the new Golden Age.

Hold this in your heart, breathe it into your being, and recognise the sense of coming home, home to the life laid out in the Divine Plan, and seeded in your soul ready for this time.

Beloved blessings, Amen.

Message of Love from Crystal Skull Susanna

Feel the resonance of my love through my energies of pink light; see the world through my energies of love and compassion.

Hear the world through the energies of love. Speak of the world through the energies of my love, and feel the resonance of the world at peace through your heart chakra, and link to all humanity, and all beings beyond.

See the love and compassion radiating from the hearts and minds of all souls, all living beings and Mother Earth, and see this radiating ball of love light energy in all its glory.

Feel the resonance of this energy and return to this sense of love and peace, compassion and understanding whenever you are drawn to do so, knowing you are adding beautifully to the love and light of All That Is anchoring in the peace across all times, levels and dimensions, world without end. Amen.

About Lindsay

My journey in this lifetime has led to the exploration of many topics including crystals, healing modalities, understanding about life in Atlantis and Lemuria, studying with the Diana Cooper School, and ultimately receiving the wonderful gift of channelled information. The beautiful energies known as The Crystal Team lovingly share their wisdoms and insights, and are available to read on www.lindsayball.co.uk

My more recent weblog www.thewayofpeace-lindsayball.co.uk is in alignment with the changing energies as the collective consciousness continues to awaken to the possibilities and potentialities of a new way of life where decisions are made for the greatest good of all, Mother Earth, and all living beings. This assists in the co-creation of a life of peace, equality, harmony, sustainability, joy and creativity, which is based on heart-centred decisions and actions made with love and compassion.

It is my passion to work towards creating a better world for this and future generations, all living beings, and to honour our home and provider Mother Earth.

Acknowledgements

My thanks and appreciation goes to all who have assisted in the publication of this book.

Thank you to all light workers, peace workers, those involved in new technologies, sustainability, renewable energy, creating a cleaner environment, and in any way working towards raising the collective consciousness and unity, supporting the co-creation of a more peaceful, joyful, just, equal, abundant, way of life on earth.

My love and gratitude to The Crystal Team for their dedication in sharing insights and information to assist us all on our individual and collective journeys, as we move towards creating Nova Earth as ordained in the Blueprint for earth. Amen.

It is an honour and a privilege to co-create the 'The Way Forward' series, and to offer these loving insights at this auspicious time on earth.

Review

This book gives a clear insight into the magical world of crystals and the important role they have, and continue to play, in the unfolding of life on earth.

The energetic connection to all things crystal supports humanity on its journey to enlightenment and the co-creation of the new era of peace, harmony, love, and joy which is prophesied for earth, and all living beings.
Highly recommended for crystal fans everywhere!

Helen Anita Grundy
Equilibrium - The Natural Health Centre

Follow www.thewayofpeace-lindsayball.co.uk for more regular updates from Lindsay and The Crystal Team

Disclaimer: The insights shared in this book and via my websites are for information purposes only; please enjoy that which resonates with you and always be reminded to seek professional assistance for any health and well-being related concerns.

Love and blessings Lindsay and The Crystal Team